Thought Styles

This book is due for return not later than the last
date stamped below, unless recalled sooner.

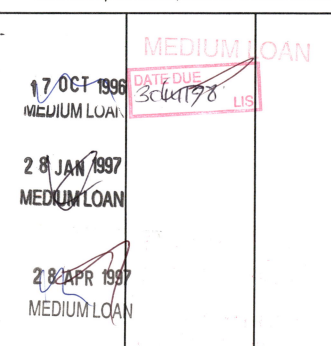

Thought Styles

Critical Essays on Good Taste

Mary Douglas

SAGE Publications

London • Thousand Oaks • New Delhi

First published 1996

 SAGE Publications Ltd
6 Bonhill Street
London EC2A 4PU

SAGE Publications Inc
2455 Teller Road
Thousand Oaks, California 91320

SAGE Publications India Pvt Ltd
32, M-Block Market
Greater Kailash – I
New Delhi 110 048

British Library Cataloguing in Publication data

A catalogue record for this book is
available from the British Library.

ISBN 0 8039 7655 0
ISBN 0 8039 7656 9 (pbk)

Library of Congress catalog record available

Typeset by Mayhew Typesetting, Rhayader, Powys
Printed in Great Britain by The Cromwell Press Ltd,
Broughton Gifford, Melksham, Wiltshire

Contents

List of Figures

Acknowledgements

The chapters in this volume have previously appeared as follows:

Chapter 1: Originally presented as the thirteenth Katharine Briggs Memorial Lecture to the Folklore Society and first published in *Folklore* 106 (1995): 1–7.

Chapter 2: 'The construction of the physician: a cultural approach to medical fashions', in S. Budd and U. Sharma (eds), *The Healing Bond: the Patient–Practitioner Relationship and Therapeutic Responsibility*. London: Routledge, 1994. pp. 24–41.

Chapter 3: 'The idea of a good pot', Tate Gallery Conference on Values in Art, 22 October 1993.

Chapter 4: 'In defence of shopping', in R. Eisendle and E. Miklautz (eds), *Produktkulturen: Dynamik und Bedeutungswendel des Konsums*. Frankfurt: Campus, 1992. pp. 95–117.

Chapter 5: Talk given in a seminar series on Consumption in the Hall of St Mary's, Oxford, organized by Marjorie Reeves and the Reverend Brian Mountford, 14 January 1991, and also discussed in a workshop at the Centre for Cultural Values, Lancaster University, 27 February 1991. It has been published as 'The consumer's conscience', in Mary Douglas, *Objects and Objections*. Toronto Semiotic Circle Monograph Series, No. 9, 1992. Toronto: Victoria College in the University of Toronto. pp. 49–65.

Acknowledgements

Chapter 6: 'The pangolin revisited: a new approach to animal symbolism', in Roy Willis (ed.), *Signifying Animals: Human Meaning in the Natural World*. London: Unwin Hyman, 1990. pp. 25–36.

Chapter 7: 'Ralph Bulmer among the master detectives', in A. Pawley (ed.), *Man and a Half: Essays in Pacific Anthropology and Ethnobiology in Honour of Ralph Bulmer*. Auckland: Polynesian Society, 1991. pp. 193–8.

Chapter 8: 'Governability: a question of culture', *Millennium: Journal of International Studies*, 1992, 22(3): 463–81.

Chapter 9: Originally delivered as the 1993 Henry Rapaport Lecture at the Jewish Theological Seminary of America, and published as 'Holy Joy: rereading Leviticus. The anthropologist and the believer', *Conservative Judaism*, 1994, XLVI (3): 3–14.

Figures 3.1–3.6 are reproduced by kind permission of the British Museum.

Introduction

These essays are on varied subjects, written for varied occasions, but they all relate to disagreement about individual likes and dislikes. The experience seems to be entirely private, a matter of palate or eye, then we discover that a lot of other people feel the same way. We have not persuaded them, nor have they persuaded us. We also agree about our disapproval of others whose reactions are different.

There is a point at which a private thought, after it has come into being, either vanishes or slots into a ready frame of stock connections, and then stays on as part of the local ambience that catches future thoughts and holds them steady. The process is culture in action. What is that frame made of? How stable can it be, how does it dissolve away? The theme follows on my reflections in *How Institutions Think* (1987).

The problem of why people reason differently belongs to the history of anthropology. It would be comforting to think that everyone who disagreed with us had a defect of reasoning. James Frazer accounted for magic by imputing haziness to the unevolved thought of primitives (1936). A less comforting side of that idea would be that people really think in such fundamentally different ways and feel so differently about the same things that there is no common ground or hope for coming to terms. Lucien Lévy-Bruhl came up with the idea that the emotional focus affects the interpretation of evidence; if primitives seem to think differently from us, it is not because they are incapable of logical deduction, but that before logical operations are brought into action there is an 'affective bias' which causes evidence and logic to be short-circuited in favour of what he called 'mystic participation' (1952). He implied that we ourselves have less of the affective bias.

If we have it at all, does our mystic participation prevent us communicating with others who do not share its concrete particularity? Maurice Leenhardt perceived Melanesian thought to be a particular kind of engagement with the world of concrete presences and emotional participation, expressive and mystical, rather than analytic (Clifford, 1982). If we cannot join the participations of others, but must needs only admire them, the outlook is dim for hopes of mutual understanding.

My suggestion is, instead of going abroad, we could start by examining the different thought styles that separate us, here at home. On a Durkheimian approach a distinctive thought style develops as the communicative genre for a social unit speaking to itself about itself, and so constituting itself. Science has its several thought styles. See for example, how Ian Hacking has dissected distinctive styles of statistics embedded in styles of government (Hacking, 1990). Among the first of these exercises in disembedding thought, Ludwik Fleck's account of the history of venereal disease in modern medicine and his description of a scientific community as a 'thought collective' (1935) is unsurpassed.

The essays in this volume stand a little to the side of the main stream of philosophy of science as they take their examples from literature and everyday life. I often hear the discouraging idea that a distinctive thought style corresponds to a historically unique bias in a particular community, itself also unique, so unique that they cannot be compared. But I am arguing that there is scope for classifying not the thought styles in themselves but the kinds of social units for which they serve as the medium of communication. How do thoughts get standardized? To answer we would have to learn to compare communities. But this requires unwonted attention paid to the community that issues its thoughts in a standardized form. The question of judgement is why people make different inferences from the same evidence, and the answer must have something to do with how cultural bias colours thought.

At the major cross-roads of life personal choice is constrained by allegiance. Loyalties are present, alignments count. Cultural theory attempts to close the chasms of relativism that open before arguments about unique meanings. However, it needs to seek a minimum basis for agreement. Here and now, in the late twentieth century, after so much sociological effort, it is still hard to muster consensus about social relations and the experience of power and authority. Here I start by assuming that there is a dimension which all communities recognize and construct: a scale that distinguishes degrees of formality. In the first essay I propose that there is a universal distinction which everyone can recognize between intimacy and formal distance. Members cannot operate in the community unless they understand the difference between vulgarity and refinement. Children learn it. Outsiders recognize it. This is the minimal starting point which I use in the first two essays.

French versions of the familiar story of Red Riding Hood reveal a verbal ritual celebrating the stages of a woman's life. Though quite bawdy in itself, it is on the polite end of the scale from vulgar to refined, compared to the rude horseplay of the equivalent rituals for boys. Once the Mother Goose stories have been read in the light of the gender celebrations of French nineteenth-century peasant life, surely folklore can never be the same. On these lines, the gamut from vulgar to refined affords an interpretive tool that could be more generally used.

The next essay, on styles of therapy, applies the same scale, from vulgar to refined, to medicine. This is an example of how cultural alignments are clarified and strengthened by being strung out on the dimension which at its most inclusive is the gamut from formal to informal, but which provides minute rules of politeness, for how to address superiors and equals, or how to choose a doctor, or a remedy. Social life is threaded and pitted with discriminations on this basis. They are not just signals of moral and political alignment, but weapons in a vigorous contest between styles of organization. Members of a community either line up in support of the hegemonic culture, whatever that may be, or they line up against it, or they have the option of going into the sidelines, without hope of influence or favour. Choosing one doctor means not choosing another, choosing one remedy means rejecting another. Any choosing 'for', is also a choosing 'against'.

The next three chapters, 3, 4 and 5, have to do with choice in domestic furnishings. Shopping is the traditional arena of choice. Hitherto the bias of market research and opinion polling has been focused on positive preferences. Protest shopping has been neglected. Not buying a particular detergent is just as significant a form of protest as not choosing a doctor. In these three essays I deploy my favourite schema, the field of force in which social environments crystallize and draw the population to one or other of four strongly marked positions. When a new private thought comes into being, it may have a chance to escape being embedded in a social institution. It will then likely pay for its originality in being forgotten. For an idea to become embedded is like a research proposal that gets funding. The sources of support are the institutions which gather the wherewithal for funding and bestow it on loyal followers. The thoughts we know about have been funded, the ones we are about to forget are having their funds withdrawn, we ourselves cut their life-lines by forgetting. The ideas we cannot understand, try as we may, ideas from foreign thought styles, are either funded in a different currency, or have been unfunded for so long that no one remembers how they once fitted into a context. The examples which best show us, we ourselves, passing adverse judgements and so killing off the unfashionable thoughts, come in the essay on bad taste (Chapter 3).

Choices between furniture and pots and pans make a light approach to a more sombre theme. For the same gamut is evident in the cultural choice between eating or abstaining from animal flesh. Abstaining raises questions for the rest of the book, questions of classification and interpretation, and the problem of metaphors. If we see a particular animal mentioned in an ancient text as an obvious source of metaphor, a lion or eagle for legitimate majesty, a wolf for illicit robbery, there is no guarantee that the issuers of the text or the people to whom it was addressed saw that animal that way. In Genesis Jacob, as he gave his sons his deathbed blessings, likened them to animals, Judah to a lion, Issachar to an ass, Benjamin to a wolf, Dan to a viper, Napthali to a deer (Genesis 49). We cannot be certain which would have been considered flattering, or whether they were prophecies of what the future held for the individual tribes. The only guarantee for interpreting metaphors comes from the mesh between what the people are doing and what they are saying. Social and literary context justify your reading.

Chapter 8 applies cultural theory to the history of ascetic movements and tries to assess the future of general vegetarianism in Europe. In any country, convention gives various reasons for counting an animal as inedible: that it is noble, like the horse, or that it is charming and attractive, like the lark, or that it is ignoble, like snakes, snails or slugs. None of them holds good abroad, where the creature avoided may be specially relished. As I have explained in Chapters 6 and 7, on animal classification, there is no general rule that will pick out anomalous animal kinds. It rests entirely on the local web of connections.

It is generally assumed that the animals which the Bible forbids are of an ignoble kind, snakes and insects, pigs and camels, squid, crabs and eels. Metaphors of evil living are adduced to justify the view. But in Chapter 9 I am boldly suggesting that there has been a long misunderstanding of the text. It puts the passage in Leviticus 11 more squarely into the larger biblical context to read the passage as saying, not that the forbidden animals are abominable, but that eating them is abominable. The main reason for including that chapter in this collection is that it describes an anthropologist's approach to foreign religions which is very similar to the approach adopted towards differences of taste and judgement.

References

Clifford, J. (1982) *Person and Myth: Maurice Leenhardt in the Melanesian World*. Berkeley, CA: University of California Press.

Douglas, Mary (1987) *How Institutions Think*. New York: Syracuse University Press.

Fleck, L. (1935) *The Genesis and Development of a Scientific Fact* (trans. 1979). Chicago: University of Chicago Press.

Frazer, J. (1936) *The Golden Bough*. London: Macmillan.

Hacking, I. (1990) *The Taming of Chance*. Cambridge: Cambridge University Press.

Lévy-Bruhl, L. (1952) 'A letter to E.E. Evans-Pritchard', *British Journal of Sociology*, III(2): 117–23.

1

The Uses of Vulgarity: a French Reading of Little Red Riding Hood

There is always a problem of how to interpret a story when it is not clear whether it is meant to be funny or tragic, and when the whole social context is missing. It must be in line with critical theory to say that when *all* you have is the story itself the meaning is whatever the reader assigns to it. In a sense you, the newest reader, become the author of the current meanings. This should be a comfort to the up-dating feminist readings of Mother Goose stories, and to psychoanalytic readings, or jazzy Monty Python style reworking, or collections of old meanings (Zipes, 1993). But it is very little comfort to old-fashioned folklorists or anthropologists who might want to know what the story originally meant to say.

The folklorists I know are mild and tolerant people. Far from them is it to impose their British, Finnish or German understandings on foreign texts. They would never wish to endorse a cultural imperialism which assumes there is only one true meaning which we happen to possess; to appropriate the sacred texts of other cultures would be abhorrent to them. But what can they do? Either they accept that the archaeology of textual meanings is impossible or they accept the transformation of one honourable profession into another, from folklore to literature, from interpretation to reading.

We cannot easily abandon the intention to interpret the

thing as it was once meant to be. I propose to borrow an idea from the work of Norbert Elias (Elias, 1978), and turn what could be called his 'distance index' into something more systematic. Behaviour and words about behaviour, the resonance between action and word, between word and body, and between body and cosmos, are anthropologists' normal material. In *The Civilizing Process* Elias emphasized the use of distance to express formality and respect. The smaller the physical distance between persons' bodies, the more the intimacy; this is the low respect end of the continuum. The greater the distance, the more the authority; this is the high respect end. The projection of the social structure on physical space is so familiar to anthropologists that it seems surprising that Elias felt he had been struck by a novel idea. It can perhaps be developed into a tool of textual criticism that will at least tell us whether a tale is more vulgar or more refined than another in the same genre. And I suggest it will help to show original contrasts between genres. I will illustrate the idea from stories about people eating people or being eaten, especially Red Riding Hood's experiences with the wolf that ate her grandmother.

Our version of Red Riding Hood

The interpretation that I will offer of Red Riding Hood will be drawn from that of the late, lamented Yvonne Verdier. She was a feminist anthropologist some of whose fieldwork was in the village of Minot, in Burgundy. Interviewing the oldest old women and taking part in farm life she gave us a version that emanates from a known and defined group. It is independent of Perrault and Grimm, French not German, rustic not urban, peasant not bourgeois, and very different from what we tell to our children.

Our version is a story about a little girl who goes to take butter and cakes to her grandmother; she meets a wolf who asks where she is going and who runs ahead and kills and eats the old lady. Disguised as the grandmother he gets into her bed before the little girl arrives. An innocent conversation takes place as the child takes stock of changes in the physical appearance of her grandmother.

> What big eyes you have, Grandmama!
> All the better to see you with, my dear.

Friendly enough, surely?

> What big ears you have, Grandmama!
> All the better to hear you with, my dear!

Still very benign! But when she says,

> What big teeth!

the wolf answers

> All the better to eat you with!

He jumps out of bed, grabs her and is just about to devour her when the wood cutter turns up in time to save the child, kill the wolf, cut open its belly and rescue the grandmother alive. The story is told with mounting excitement between teller and listener, climaxing with a sudden pounce and a flurry of giggles.

We may still ask why we consider the story of Red Riding Hood suitable for small children. A young girl is attacked by a wild beast and only saved in the nick of time. The animal has already killed and eaten her grandmother. Does this present an antique parallel to modern media violence (Duclos, 1994)? Are the stories in the Strewel Peter collection really terrifying *grand guignol*? Is Sweeney Todd suitable for children? Or is it funny? How do we know? To be sure, there are conventions for recognizing humour. But the conventions are local and fairly

3

esoteric. A clown has baggy trousers and a red nose, the sadder he looks, the funnier is the clowning. If we know the conventions we can recognize that a narrative has been marked off from everyday reality. But what if we don't?

There are many fascinating Bantu stories about cannibals, male and female (Paulme, 1976). Anyone travelling in West or Central Africa will be sure to encounter contemporary tales about white men who go round at night in lorries picking up little black children and taking them off to be butchered and eaten. If anyone questions the validity of the myth, they are given compelling circumstantial evidence. Go to any European hotel, and see for yourself the vast quantities of meat served there regularly, grilled or stewed or in sausages. How else but by cooking their fellow humans can the whites maintain such an extravagant carnivorous cuisine? The culinary details of sausages and grill carry conviction. Are the stories jokes or anticolonial propaganda? They compare with other accusations of cannibalism, such as the medieval Christian allegation that the Jews performed child sacrifice and child eating, or the ancient Israelites' rebukes to Canaanites offering child sacrifice to Moloch. A context of hostility allows us to read outrage and disgust, a context of nursery bedtime fun swivels the whole meaning round. But supposing we have not got the context of laughter, how can we know from the text alone?

Sometimes we can recognize verbal framing devices. Red Riding Hood is separated off from realism and the violence of everyday first by the conventional 'Once upon a time . . .' opening which declares a world of fantasy. The story then unfolds quite naturalistically until the wolf meets her on the path and speaks to her. Then the second clue, a talking wolf is in a class with the talking bears in Goldilocks, the cat who advises Dick Whittington, the hen in the Beanstalk world who shouts warnings to Jack, the wolf who threatens the three little pigs, and so on. By the very fact of his speech the wolf is situated in a world of fantasy. Third, there is the happy ending, which can be anticipated with its many repetitions, the death of the wolf and the resuscitation of the grandmother. We can see that Red Riding Hood properly told is a story that Nanny would have no reason to ban from the nursery.

In the French versions which provided the material for Grimm and Perrault Red Riding Hood seems to me to be very funny. But how do I know? Even in our own culture, with full context available, we cannot always be sure whether something is a joke or a mistake. Notoriously no one can see a joke against themselves. If we agree that there is no way of being sure that a joke is intended, it might be better to avoid thinking of funny/not funny as a set of absolute contrasts. Relatively light, and relatively serious, may be more interesting categories of judgement. My purpose is to show that even if we did not have some contextual evidence about how the French versions were told, we could still say a lot about the genre from the details about bodily indignity and indecency.

Inversion

First I would like to dispose of the idea that 'inversion' is a helpful clue to interpretation. I once argued that the social situation provides the context for seeing a joke (Douglas, 1975). I claimed that the social context gives licence for the laugh: if the context is wrong, the same event will just not be funny. For recognizing 'the right context' I took the old idea that a joke has the structure of an inversion, I added the idea that the inversion can be read as an analogy of the social situation, and added one more principle: that if the social structure is of a kind in which reversal is thinkable, then the latent joke is licensed and everyone can laugh; but if the social situation is tense with anxiety and fear, any expression of reversal is too dangerous, and the latent joke will be rejected. I still believe that social awareness flips the joke into and out of the danger areas. This is hard for folklorists, since archaic texts usually have few supporting clues about the needs of the social situation. It would be a hard message for conversation analysts if they were to limit the context to first-hand witness of verbal communication. However, I am hoping to contribute to the movement to extend the range of interest in social context and non-verbal communication. I mean to offer a way in which social norms and structures can be taken systematically into account.

The trouble is that, without those clues from the social situation, possible inversions lie in wait for the interpreter at every step. It is not enough to say that we can recognize a joke because it inverts the order of things. Latent jokes are always present. Inversion is a great religious theme: what is impossible for humans is possible for God; he brings the powerful down and raises up the humble. Inversion is so much everywhere that if it was the sole clue to the presence of a joke we would never stop laughing. Furthermore, recognizing inversion in a foreign culture is not so easy. Anyone who thinks we can recognize inversion unequivocally is assuming that norms are beyond and above culture, and that is anathema for social anthropologists.

Following Lévi-Strauss's teaching, many have tried to read myths as inverted structures. The tales that we try to interpret in terms of people's institutions often turn out to be not elaborations upon real life, past or present, but inside out and upside down versions of daily practice. But

6

what sort of comfort is that? What does it tell us about the meaning of the story? Max Muller was embarrassed on behalf of the Greek gods whose nobility and dignity he championed, by the stories of divine cannibalism. Kronus swallowing his children seemed to him to be a vulgar and ungodlike way to behave. He came out of the dilemma by claiming that the swallowing stories were not ugly evidence of primitive cannibalism, but beautiful allegories of nature: Kronus, understood as the god of time, swallowed up the day (and at dawn regurgitated). But if some are nature myths, why not all? The interpretation came in for plenty of mockery, with Little Red Riding Hood parodied by E.B. Tylor (1871) as the goddess of dawn.

Would it have helped Muller to say that tales of cannibal gods are presenting exactly the opposite of normal divine behaviour? It is not so easy to use the idea, because with gods what is the right way up? How are we to know whether to read the story the right way up or upside down? Is Red Riding Hood to be taken as an inversion of everyday behaviour or the norm? Was Moloch's hunger for human babies an inversion of Israelite behaviour? Were the Canaanites portrayed by these stories as inverted worshippers? It is tempting to read the general anti-idolatry theme of the Bible into the message that false gods consume children and the true God of Israel protects children (Douglas, 1993). However, my conclusion is that inversion is not delicately calibrated enough for our purposes.

In Adam Kuper's account of Southern Bantu cannibal tales we learn that cannibals are contrasted implicitly with the good ancestral spirits, who protect people and foster human health and fertility. Cannibals are also directly contrasted to human beings (Kuper, 1987). Unlike humans,

7

who live in settlements, the cannibal lives in a cave in the bush, like a wild animal. The cannibal hunts human beings (whom he calls 'game') and cooks human meat together with animal meat. The cannibal is also very large and very hairy, with oversize genitals. Though more like an animal, he or she often has one huge leg instead of two, or only one toe: in Bantu lore one-leggedness is a characteristic of intermediaries between man and the spirits. Ancestor spirits may live in the sky or below the ground, and may intervene in the form of snakes or birds. When people escape from cannibals, they often do so disguised as birds or snakes (Kuper, 1987).

Clearly the Bantu ogres are not like normal human beings, nor are they like ancestors; their habitat is turned in the other direction, towards land instead of towards sky. The ogre is not an opposite, but an intermediary, not necessarily between just two points but possibly on some range of which we only have a small part. 'Inversion' does not allow of this triple set of comparisons. The movement of the three genres goes in three directions: up towards spirit and sky, down towards earthbound humans, and further down towards underground caves. Three kinds of discourse are thus distinguished, that of everyday life, between humans, that between humans and ancestors, in prayer and sacrifice, and that between humans and ogres, dissolving in laughter. Yes, the stories as told to children go into gory details of children being swallowed or entering the body of the ogre via the anus, and travelling around the inside of the ogre, with indecent jokes and gales of laughter about the state of his innards, before they are rescued. You can't get much more disrespectful. In Bantu communicative genres the ogre is definitely treated to the low respect end of the continuum between spatial contiguity and spatial distance.

Dignity, decency and distance

A 'dignity register' would be a good name for using distance from the actual body as an expression of respect. The gamut between respect and intimacy projects a spatial indicator of social usage. Linguists have observed similarly that distance in language from bodily function and bodily parts projects respect and disrespect. The distance indicator can carry complex information, not just about a single value for respect, but highly differentiated relationships, once the north and south axis and east/west are taken into account.

The distance indicator that Elias observed for courtly behaviour in sixteenth-century Europe has been commonly reported in anthropological studies from the time of Durkheim. All communicative behaviour deploys an extended analogic structure, and the body is always more or less engaged. The patterning of respect on distance is only one dimension. There is theoretically no end to modelling. Roland Barthes demonstrated the fine degrees of difference between occasions that are signalled by fine degrees in dress (Barthes, 1967). Systematically graded differences in dress, food and speech correspond to systematically graded differences in social relations.

Can we not use this spontaneous grading to solve some problems of interpreting a text? It is not a difficult or ambiguous thing to recognize the coarse end of a scale that goes from gross to refined, or from material to spiritual, or from earthy to heavenly, from impure to pure, and so on. Everyone does it all the time. Done with care it can help to relate one genre to others in the same scale, and one narrative in a genre to others more refined or more vulgar. This, I suggest, is a much more instructive exercise than trying to distinguish between funny and not funny.

Every community discriminates in its references to bodily behaviour between spiritual and gross, respectful and disrespectful, regular and grotesque, gentle and violent. This goes on for as many dimensions as interest the community in question. We can't expect to notice all the dimensions, but in any one case we could establish the gradient between vulgar and refined. You can call this the distance, or the dignity, or the spirituality index. One end of the spirituality index makes reference to bodily functions and bodily parts that would not be acceptable in polite company. What is and is not acceptable can only be determined by the mythologist's reading in the other genres. We expect the scale of bodily reference to vary according to an unspoken scale of honour and dishonour. The gradients in that scale point to the meaning of the stories.

The French version: *Le Petit Chaperon Rouge*

According to the most frequently recorded form of the original Red Riding Hood tale, both the wolf and the little girl eat parts of the grandmother (Verdier, 1980). Learning this was for me a shock. How could the story about that sweet child have to do with her drinking bowls of her own grandmother's blood? Or eating her grandmother's sexual organs and breasts? It is even more of a shock than discovering that none of the original versions describes her hood as red. Admittedly the child does not know that the soup that the wolf gives her is made from her grandmother's blood, but none the less, she is an unwitting cannibal.

Another shock is that though our versions focus on the wolf as a child-eating monster, according to Yvonne

Verdier's interpretation based on an analysis of all the available French versions, his role is quite incidental and unimportant. The Brothers Grimm have done something drastic to the story; it has been gentrified almost out of recognition.

In the original French versions the conversation between the wolf and the little girl is laced with sexy innuendo: he asks her to get into bed with him, and she complies quite happily. In bed together, her surprised remarks on her grandmother's body ('How big' . . . ! How hairy . . . ! How strong . . . !) elicit lewd answers, starting with 'All the better to . . .'. Their far from innocent pillow-talk is not at all what Nanny would tolerate. The denouement in the French versions does not have recourse to a heroic male figure. There is no woodcutter to do battle with the fearsome beast, kill him, slit him open so that the granny can step out, alive and well. The young French heroine escapes by her own ingenuity and with the help of other female characters. When she gets frightened she tries to get out of the bed. The wolf refuses to let her go. The wolf asks is she not warm and comfortable in bed? She says she must do *pipi*, urgently. He tells her: If you must, you can do it in the bed. But she insists that she can't, and finally they hit on a compromise: he ties a rope to her leg, and holds on to his end of it so she cannot get away. But once outside she frees herself, slips the rope round the trunk of a tree, then makes a dash for the river. On the other bank stand the washerwomen. They throw a sheet into the water, and pull her safely across. When the wolf discovers the ruse, he chases her to the river bank, and tries to persuade the washerwomen to bring him across by the same means. They seem to comply. They throw the sheet in for him, but once he is on it, they let go and he is drowned.

11

The feminine order

The language of the French versions suggests we should be imagining a much older girl than our picture books show – *ma petite fille* means both 'my little girl' and 'my grand-daughter'. Yvonne Verdier suggested the story made more sense if she was a girl approaching puberty, this for reasons that will appear.

In all the French versions of the story when the wolf meets the girl he asks her which way she is going to her grandmother's house. Will she take the path of needles or the path of pins? Different versions put different answers into her mouth. The answer she gives does not matter, the important thing is the mention of the two paths. Peasant women in nineteenth-century France, when these stories were collected, had an informal system of age-classes. The stages of a woman's life were distinguished by the symbolism of pins and needles. Pins are easy to use but only make temporary fastenings, needles are employed with skill and perseverance, they make permanent ties. Pins have no opening, putting a thread through the eye of a needle has a simple sexual connotation. The pin can be a symbol of the virgin intact, the needle is the adult woman. Courting girls receive pretty pins as gifts from admirers, or throw pins into the wishing well. The choice between pins and needles is in all the versions before Perrault and Grimm tidied them up to be suitable for our nurseries. Any interpretation that omits that detail is suspect.

The mention of pins and needles would alert the French listener to expect a story referring to sex and to the sequence of roles that the female child will go through in her life. After puberty the young village girl used to go with her cohort to another village to spend a happy winter season with the dressmaker. Staying in the dressmaker's house was like a period of ritual seclusion, a light-hearted time of initiation into girlhood. It was more like a finishing school in which they became sophisticated, learnt the rudiments of sewing. Though Verdier does not say it in so many words, the reference to sophistication gained suggests that it was when they learn how to look their best, how to deal with admirers, become wise about sex and how to avoid conception. Living together away from home for the first time the girls formed the solidary ties that would last through their lives. Their home-coming in the spring had its own ceremonious implications. They were deemed then to be the right age to enjoy the frivolous period of courtship, the time of pins and temporary attachments.

The passage of the seasons provides a parallel to the maturing of the girls. They would have worked hard in the fields all the summer, in the winter they went away to rest from those hard labours and to meet the girls from other villages and make friendships that last a lifetime. After the giddy May festivities they would have matured to womanhood, marriage, the great permanent attachment, the serious work of needles. Finally they would grow old, too old to be able to thread a needle (in both senses), like the grandmother. By omitting the wolf's question about pins or needles, the versions we have received have lost the framing cue for setting the stories in the ritualized passage of the female generations.

What really happened

Yvonne Verdier argues that there is nothing in Red Riding Hood to indicate signs of myth inversion. In her grand-mother's house the girl conducts herself as she would in a normal kitchen.

Having arrived at her grandmother's house, the little girl is
invited by the wolf to take some refreshment; or even it is she
who, upon entering, declares that she is hungry, then thirsty
(then sleepy). He tells her to have some of the meat in the
cupboard, or the chest or the larder and to pour herself a glass
of wine. The scene is intimate, domestic, the wolf watches her
from the bed as she busies herself. She goes through all the
actions of preparing a meal, gets out the ingredients for the
meal, lights the fire, stirs the cooking pots . . .

Let us remember the actions of the wolf. He arrives, kills
the grandmother, partly consumes her, bleeds her, puts the
blood aside in a bottle, a glass, a dish, a pot, a basin, a bowl,
and keeps the flesh – the term used – which he stores away
like other food in the box, or larder or cupboard. In one
version it is the head which he puts on a plate . . . (Verdier,
1980, p. 41)

Except for the presence of the wolf, this is definitely not an
inverted version of everyday comportment. That being so,
how is it to be interpreted? Was life so rough that little
girls really attacked their grandmothers in nineteenth-
century France?

Robert Darnton, a historian who has paid attention to
these Mother Goose stories, has ventured a general comparison between German and French folk tales. He finds
more cunning and humour on the French side, more
numbskull Simple Simon types of heroes on the German
side, dealing with more terror and fantasy. Since he finds
that the central feature of this story is that Red Riding
Hood cheats the wolf at the end, he adds it to his category
of French folk tales which extol roguery. And he will have
nothing to say for inversion; if the story characters are
unkind to each other, that must have been the way it was
at the time of their telling:

'. . . If the world is cruel, the village nasty, and mankind
infested with rogues, what is one to do?' (Darnton, 1984)

Following Yvonne Verdier, we will agree that there is no
inversion, and that the tale has to do with everyday
matters, but the story unfolds a hitherto unsuspected
meaning.

Yvonne Verdier conducted field research among the old
women in the village of Minot in Burgundy (Verdier,
1979). She argued that the succession of roles in the
feminine world is the known backdrop to a range of
Mother Goose stories about blood, sex and rivalry. Not just
the role transfers between generations of women, but
beliefs about female physiology have to be understood.
Unlike men, whose bodies are set on a steady course
through life, alienated from the cycles of nature, those
women know that their bodies swing them between reason
and emotion on a monthly programme in harmony with
the seasons of the year. The women's physiological month
reproduces in small Nature's whole year. The days of
menstruation correspond to the month of May, when
nature goes into a state of fermentation, birthing, hatching,
budding, mushrooming in rich profusion.

Accepting the reality of the connection between their
bodily cycles and those of nature, women impose rules
upon themselves during their own monthly period of
fermentation. Fearing that they could contaminate other
fermentation processes menstruating women avoid touching wine vessels or going into the wine cellar, or touching
pork in brine, lest by contagion with their state of fermentation it ferments and turns bad. These are responsibilities
of women that demonstrate their close affinity to nature;
their work is giving birth, feeding, washing and caring for
the body. With all of this the cohort of young girls must
also be taught that they will advance to take over the
reproductive roles of their seniors.

The Mother Goose stories provide an informal reference

to the seasonal and life-cycle rituals, which for the girls culminate in the May Day celebrations. The actual arrangements for training the girls and for ordaining their place in the social order are supported by the rituals of first communion and marriage, a liturgy for which the stories, if that is what they are, provide ad hoc commentaries. According to Verdier we should not look for a direct narrative meaning to justify the stories of Sleeping Beauty or Red Riding Hood. To ask what the stories mean as stories hardly makes sense. They have some entertainment value, but that is because of the reference to well-known rituals and statuses. Their meaning is in the play upon the current pattern of feminine roles and upon the conflicts and tensions inherent therein. It is a joke, and at the same time it is not a joke but true that little girls will always grow up to go into their grandmothers' house and consume the substance of their mothers' mothers.

Puzzles raised by narrativization

The so-called folk tales have been wrongly assimilated to our own idea of narrative. By being treated as legends or folk tales, and by being endowed with a modest equivalence with those of ancient Greek gods and the Teutonic sagas – even by the mere fact of having been collected as stories – they have been laid open to mis-understanding. Forcibly narrativized, Verdier found these tales to be more like a genre of little proverbs, games, lampoons, limericks, jokey moral lessons. In her view they never were full-blown stories with beginnings, middles and ends, but have been forced by nineteenth-century folklorists into the narrative genre. It is doubtful whether there is any other genre in our culture that corresponds to such little bits and pieces. Scraps of songs and sayings making a salacious commentary upon the feminine order, they are too fragile to bear by themselves the freight of meaning with which they are credited. Without knowing the context of action and institutions, there is no way to interpret the stories, and when the context is given, they are not so much stories as verbal rites.

The stories, as Verdier interprets them, are about and for women who live in villages strictly divided into male and female spheres. Her book about such a village has practically nothing to say about the men. They appear only as shadowy background figures, utterly dependent on women who bring them into the world as babies, and see them out of it when they prepare the corpses for burial. In the women's culture, women are at the centre of the universe, the men at the periphery. Women are in tune with nature and the seasons, and have cosmic responsibilities. In a real sense they have created a world that reverses the world of men, not merely at the level of the domestic house, but through their association with the phases of the moon and the cycle of vegetation.

In the opposite world of men there are men's life-cycle rituals, coarser than the coarsest of the versions of Red Riding Hood. The style in itself marks the difference between male and female spheres. In the village of Minot the annual pig-killings were the occasion of hilarious scatologic rites that left the little boys in no doubt about their future sexual roles. Stories about the female child appropriating the sexual parts of the grandmother are matched on the male side by the pantomime of filling the little boys' pockets with pigs' testicles. The contrast between the medium of instruction is striking. If we thought that the original stories of the little girl's cannibal feast and the titillating scene of her in bed with the wolf were crude, they are much more refined than the counterpart lessons for the boys. The medium speaks for the domestic scope of the woman compared with the men's work on the farm and with animals. After all, the feminine version is only verbal, the masculine version is a vulgar mime. The little girl politely drinks the blood and eats the meat, she has cooked it over the fire and served it in bowls and dishes, taken out of cupboards. Her lesson is just a bit of a story, the other half is told when the young boy is chased around the farmyard, bleeding pig's entrails thrown at him, real pig's innards on his head and in his clothes, amid the teasing laughter of the farming neighbourhood who attend the pig-killing as if it were a major ceremony.

Some of the meaning lies in the contrast between points on the dignity scale within the stories, and also between the genres. The French boys are put lower than the girls (as in our nursery rhymes about girls being made of sugar and spice, and boys of frogs and snails); the man-eating ogres get their meaning from their placing on this scale below the profane life of humans, who get more of their own meaning by being placed below the sacred life of ancestral spirits.

The vigour and realism of the teaching of sex roles in the evocation of the respective scenes of work is a far cry from the desiccated sex instruction in our schools. Yvonne Verdier herself has commented (1980) on the defeminization of modern culture which has made it so difficult to think about femininity at all, and so has made it difficult to recognize these stories as teaching about gender.

The lesson for the would-be mythologist or folklorist is that the story is a comment on something that is currently happening. Before mythology developed as a science about words, this is what many myth-like stories would have been. When a myth seems to be an inverted version of another myth, two fields of action will always be self-defined by reference to each other. In the ogre tales of the Southern Bantu the profane life of humans contrasts with that of the ancestral spirits, and ogres are contrasted with both. The main novelty of this approach is to seek the interpretation from outside the verbal story. The words of the tale are oblique commentary on standardized actions, employing several registers, one resonating against the other. Here I am indebted to Anita Jacobson-Widding's rich and original adaptation (Jacobson-Widding, 1990) of Paul Ricoeur's analysis of levels of discourse (Ricoeur, 1979). The actions on which the Bantu ogre tales comment are sacrificial actions, offerings of slain domestic animals to ancestors: the ancestors protect humans, the ogres eat them. Detailing the indecent topography of internal organs contributes to the entertainment value of the tales, and makes the same point about relative dignity as the graded difference in physicality in the treatment of boys and girls in Minot. Ancestors are spiritual beings, ogres are gross creatures; girls are sheltered, protected from the real rough stuff of life, which boys must manfully confront in all its bloody, physical vulgarity.

For there to be mythology at all, or ritual at all, the culture will be formed around some grand central act which integrates the different forms of life. The central facts of existence will not be the same for men and women. For the women's culture in Minot the cosmogenic acts were giving birth, and burial, celebrated by the christenings, marriages and funerals in which women played a central role. More private events underpinning the whole system were their own personal arrivals at puberty, their menstrual cycles, pregnancies, miscarriages and menopause. At the centre of the interpretation there is the physical model of their being, congruent with the cycle of nature.

19

Acknowledgement

This essay is a tribute to the late Yvonne Verdier, whose fieldwork in a French village and whose analysis of the Red Riding Hood stories and criticism are the basis of the interpretation given here.

References

Barthes, Roland (1967) *Le Système de la mode*. Paris: Seuil.
Darnton, Robert (1984) *The Cat Massacre and Other Episodes in French Cultural History*. New York: Vintage Books, Random House. pp. 29–55.
Douglas, Mary (1975) 'Jokes', in *Implicit Meanings*. London: Routledge. pp. 90–116.
Douglas, Mary (1993) *In the Wilderness: the Doctrine of Defilement in the Book of Numbers*. Sheffield: Academic Press.
Duclos, Denis (1994) *Le Loup-Garou: la fascination de la violence dans la culture Americaine*. Paris: La Decouverte.
Elias, Norbert (1978) *The Civilizing Process*. Oxford: Basil Blackwell.
Jacobson-Widding, Anita (1990) 'The shadow as an expression of individuality in Congolese conceptions of personhood', in M. Jackson and I. Karp (eds), *Personhood and Agency: the Experience of Self and Other in African Cultures*. Uppsala: Acta Universitatis Upsaliensis.
Kuper, Adam (1987) *South Africa and the Anthropologist*. London: Routledge and Kegan Paul. p. 170.
Marriott, McKim (1976) 'Hindu transactions, diversity without dualism', in Bruce Kapferer (ed.), *Transaction and Meaning: Directions in the Anthropology of Exchange and Symbolic Behaviour*. Philadelphia: ISHI.
Paulme, Denise (1976) *La Mère Dévorante: essai sur la morphologie des contes Africains*. Paris: Gallimard.
Ricoeur, Paul (1979) 'The model of the text: meaningful action considered as text', in P. Rabinow and W. Sullivan (eds), *Interpretive Social Science*. Berkeley, CA: University of California Press.
Tylor, E.B. (1871) *Primitive Culture*. London: John Morris.
Verdier, Yvonne (1979) *Façons de dire, façons de faire: la laveuse, la couturière, la cuisinière*. Paris: Gallimard.
Verdier, Yvonne (1980) 'Le Petit Chaperon Rouge dans la tradition orale', *Le Débat*, 3: 31–56.
Zipes, Jack (ed.) (1993) *The Trials and Tribulations of Little Red Riding Hood*. London: Routledge.

2

The Choice Between Gross and Spiritual: Some Medical Preferences

The social construction of the physician

Some friends explain their preference for complementary medicine by saying either that it is 'holistic' or that it respects spiritual values, or both. Here I propose to put this preference in the context of a widespread leaning towards what I will call 'gentleness'. There have always been some people concerned for animal welfare, but now that concern is widespread. There have always been vegetarians, but good restaurants did not always offer a vegetarian menu, as they now are obliged to do if they want to stay in business. New religions depict a compassionate image of God. In a quasi-religious mood, environmentalists try to make us sensitive to nature's needs. Alternative medicine invokes tender sensibilities on behalf of the body. There has always been alternative or complementary medicine but now the sheer numbers of its followers are impressive, and increasing (Sermeus, 1987). Animals, religion, ecology and medicine: there is a case for studying them together under a single rubric, the option for gentleness.

A word about the term 'gentleness' is in order. Of course it is relative. Some forms of complementary medicine are pretty brutal, like chiropractice, and some traditional medication is painless. But surely we can agree that cutting up flesh and bone or drawing blood are violent therapies compared with remedies coming in the form of perfumes and oils, and that manipulation is less intrusive than the surgeon's knife. Acupuncture involves needle pricks sited away from the painful region, which do not hurt or even draw blood. Laying on of hands relieves pain without so much as touching the sufferer's skin. These are the new style of therapy, light oils from flowers and seeds to pamper the tired muscles, hypnotic trance to unknot deep worry, infusions of herbs to invigorate the spirit. As to diagnosis, it does no violence to the patient's bodily privacy. Because the state of the whole is manifest in its parts, the patient does not even need to undress. The global condition can be assessed through the eye, or the foot.

Though there is the possibility that the therapist too is kinder and more sympathetic, this will not do for an explanation of the preference. Much more relevant is the kind of theory that the therapist will invoke – global, holistic, spiritual, rather than local, partial and physical. Here I am particularly interested in the construction of the therapist as a guide to a different reality. The argument will be that two polarized types of therapy contain in their mutually opposed imagery two types of therapist. If we are interested in the bond between patient and doctor we must be interested in the way these constructions are made.

In 'The social construction of the patient' Claudine Herzlich and Janine Pierret (1985) present a perspective in which it is wrong to take disease to be a person's bodily condition alone. 'A person's experiences and his lay conceptions of sickness cannot be separated from macro-social phenomena.' I am saying the same about the healing bond. They go on to describe how the idea of sickness has been constructed in historic times and different places, in each case as an integral part of a world view. It should hardly be necessary to say that the healing bond is socially patterned too, and that social patterns can and should be studied in a holistic framework.

Holism

Although complementary is now the preferred term, there is a sense in which the old name of 'alternative' was right in so far as this therapeutic effort caters to a different kind of demand for health care, coming from a different source, bearing a different flag. It is alternative in the full counter-cultural sense, 'spiritual' in contrast to 'material'. Consequently strictly medical comparisons afford too narrow a basis for interpreting the key word, 'holism'. Present day medical holism is a philosophy of the body which does not grow out of the history of Western medicine. Otherwise you might say that our family doctor takes a holistic view of medicine. The smallest ailment, and she is ready to think ahead to its furthest possible repercussions through the whole range of bodily parts and medical knowledge. Consult her about a swollen shin bone, and she immediately anticipates a thrombosis; go to her with ear ache and she warns against danger of a tumour on the brain; call about your feet and she suspects possible parkinsonism. I personally appreciate having the diagnostic resources of Western medicine placed at my disposal. But this is not at all what is meant by medical holism. Our doctor's holism stops at the boundaries of the body and stays within the boundaries of the medical profession, whereas holistic medicine takes global account of the patient's whole personality and spiritual environment.

Western medicine over its history has gradually separated itself from spiritual matters. In a pluralist democracy the varied religious beliefs of the population must be respected. It would be improper for a medical practitioner to foist his own religious views on his patients. Religion was split off from medicine, psychic troubles from bodily ones, then the treatment of one limb from another, flesh from bone, skin from sub-cutaneous, organs from each other, one virus distinguished from another, and diseases, cross-cutting. As its history of research has been a process of specializing, so now the body itself is parcelled out among a host of specialists. It all comes together in a general theory of living beings, but that does not take account of the psyche. The complementary medicine that is offered as an alternative is neither encroaching on the churches nor offering to its patients the opportunity of embracing an alternative religious cult. It draws on ancient theories of how living beings are related to the cosmos, and a set of theories about the connection between psychic and physical existence: it is, in short, a cultural alternative to Western philosophic traditions.

Personal preference is not much of an explanation when one theory about what the world is like and how bodies behave opposes another. When the same population is divided in its adherence to one or the other world-view, cultural conflict is present. As the people hear the terms of the conflict, competition between cultural principles spreads; soon no one will be able to stay neutral as to meat-eating, or religion, or concern for the environment. Even medicine may become a ground for testing allegiance.

Spiritual versus material values

When I ask my friends to tell me what they mean by saying that they prefer a medical tradition that is more spiritual, they answer with a series of contrasts. The idea of spirituality in medical practice is contrasted in these conversations with materiality, physicality, violence. My other friends, who use conventional therapies, rebuke me for accepting the contrast: how can modern Western medicine be more physical, materialist or violent? But the contrast is not absurd. We have just specified the relatively incorporeal treatments which earn alternative therapies the adjective of gentle.

The contrast of spiritual and material is used in a medical context to contrast with or to complement physical needs and physicalist remedies. The claim that the new therapeutic tradition is spiritual would be valid in so far as it uses a range of symbolism that goes beyond the clinic to embrace the whole person in the whole universe. In a political context, the label 'material' becomes a criticism of holders of wealth and power. What the powerful wealthy say in defence of their ways is likely to be judged materialist; the other label, 'spiritual', is appropriated by the cultural critics for their own preferences: by the logic of opposition spiritual is incompatible with accumulating power or wealth. A preacher who makes a fortune tends to be suspected of materialist objectives.

There are many other contexts in which objects and conduct are ranked on a scale from material to spiritual. Gross/subtle, vulgar/refined, rough/smooth, harsh/gentle, brutal/tender, mechanical/personal, divine/human, pure/impure are universal forms of evaluation. Between science and the humanities we use the scale of hard/soft. Tension between material and spiritual values is always present. What I am calling the option for gentleness is a surfacing of a new trend, against the material, against vulgar, harsh, rough, hard, brutal, mechanical, and impure, complementary to a preference for spirituality.

In certain phases of human history, or in certain segments of society, the option for spirituality becomes an irresistible demand. We should make a first attempt to lay a trail that will find connections between the present option, and other such movements. The rejection of animal sacrifice in early Hinduism and the still vital Hindu movement towards ritual purity and against bloodshed is a vivid example. The debate conducted between Greek philosophers in the first centuries BC against cruelty to animals, including eating or sacrificing them, is another example. By reflecting on previous movements in the same direction, contemporary cultural conflicts about the treatment of the body, the environment and the animals can be seen as a total social phenomenon.

The challenge to medical anthropology

Any civilization that takes pride in its medicine has its own diagnostic classifications. The practitioners in an African country, the Lele, class swellings of all kinds together, which means that boils and abscesses come under the same general rubric as swollen bellies and pregnancies, all caused by fertility spirits. The same people consider that pulmonary complaints are due to a tendency for ribs to get crossed and to rub against one another, causing wheezing sounds; they diagnose certain stomach pains as caused by the liver refusing to lie flat in its proper place. In the Punjab the symptoms of stress are described as a sinking of the heart (Krause, 1989). In the history of modern medicine there were stages in which the position of organs was a principal cause of disorder. Female hysteria, for example, was thought to be caused by the womb wandering away from base. But if we were consistently to try to trace differences in the exotic medical theory by relating them to

26

earlier phases in the growth of our own, the conclusion is prejudged: the other medicine, alternative to our own, is bound to be found primitive, despised and misjudged as an early stage of evolution.

Such a condescending conclusion would be entirely false, as there is no reason to think that other medical practices ever belonged to the same kind of process as early modern medicine, to say nothing of being set on the same evolutionary path. There is always the problem of finding the right diagnostic levels for comparison. When a patient tells a modern doctor that he suffers from heartburn, the doctor does not take the description for diagnosis. Some mental troubles are currently diagnosed in Western medicine as due to physical pressure on the brain; 'foreign bodies' or 'water' can mysteriously cause pain by getting into the knee. Some kind of reality is being described by patient or doctor in terms that are technical or metaphoric, but the comparison of two medical systems has to find its way past the convenient terminology to the underlying theory which the doctor taps in making his diagnosis. Constructing a spirituality index would be a possible route for establishing comparisons.

The preference for the more spiritual quality over the more material is not an isolated choice, and each choosing has repercussions. If everyone in the community comes to prefer the spiritual, it will be seen more widely as more valuable, and the rest of the value system will adapt. This becomes a particularly influential pressure when the pattern of pure and impure situations works itself into the judgements on desirable employment and desirable marriage alliance. In Hindu India, for example, every kind of transaction is rated for its relative gain or loss of spirituality for the transactors. In the process a commonly agreed standard of ritual purity emerges. This is not first and foremost a matter for the philosophers, for the rating goes on in regular everyday thought and practice, and the philosophers justify or explain it afterwards.

In Hindu India

According to McKim Marriott (1976) the Hindu purity code provides a graduated scale of values on which every kind of object can be graded. The spiritual end of the scale includes the more refined objects, the subtler media; the material end of the scale has the gross, lower, less refined, more tangible objects. Knowledge counts as subtler than money, but money is subtler than grain or land, grain or land is not so gross as cooked food or garbage. Shedding blood or touching dead flesh is the grossest of all. The judgement of subtlety is not arbitrary, for it depends upon the possibilities of transformation.

> Indian thought understands subtler substance-codes as emerging through processes of maturation or (what is considered to be the same thing) cooking. Thus subtler essences may sometimes be ripened, extracted, or distilled out of grosser ones (as fruit comes from plants, nectar from flowers, butter from milk); and grosser substance-codes may be generated or precipitated out of subtler ones (as plants come from seed, faeces from food). (Marriott, 1976, p. 110)

Every kind of transaction between castes is given a ranking, according to whether the giver is passing on gross or subtle substances to the receiver.

The caste ranking is like a ladder, higher castes are purer, and lower castes less pure. The offering and receiving of cooked food is the testing ground for claimed rank in the purity code. In this superb article Marriott analyses the strategies by which givers and receivers maintain or improve their position on the ladder of purity.

28

It may seem remote and exotic to us here and now, but it would be self-deception not to recognize the Indian code as a consistently developed variant of the common model of classifying by degrees of spirituality.

French good taste

To bring the topic nearer to home we can consider Pierre Bourdieu's theory of aesthetic judgement (1979). For market researchers it has the practical advantage of predicting the choices made in different sectors of the French populace according to the distribution of what he called 'symbolic capital'. This is defined by contrast with economic capital. In practical terms symbolic capital means the investment made in training the judgement in matters educational, aesthetic, religious, ideological, metaphysical and so on. Basically symbolic capital can be represented as an investment in education that will yield income over time. It is possible to acquire it without special education if a person can establish a claim to intellectual or spiritual ascendancy. A preacher with direct revelation, or a healer, holds symbolic capital. It requires some kind of legitimacy, some kind of acceptability, but once it is there, it confers legitimacy on the judgements of its possessor. A church minister need not have years of seminary training to back his claims to a special relation with God, but if those claims are accepted in his congregation, the acceptance endows him with symbolic capital. The argument runs as follows:

1 Those who are well endowed with both economic and symbolic capital can call the tune for the reigning fashion in the arts. They are exemplified by the French Haute Bourgeoisie, represented in the liberal professions, in

medicine and the law. In other words they form and conform to the tastes of the establishment.

2 In contrast there are sectors of the population possessed only of economic capital, that is new money without education. Lacking trained aesthetic judgement, and lacking social legitimation, their opinions on art have no legitimacy and tend to be greeted with derision. They are unlikely to be able to create a new movement of taste.

3 Other sectors have only symbolic capital and nothing else. They will be the radicalized intellectuals, the patrons of the Left Bank theatre, concerts and art galleries, writers and readers of critical theory and philosophical commentary. They love to mock the pretensions of the other culture-bearers, and define themselves against the established taste.

The trouble with Bourdieu's model is that it is so French. It is just as firmly rooted in the perspective of the nineteenth- and twentieth-century French bourgeoisie as the Hindu purity scale is rooted in India. For all that, his schematization of artistic taste is very suggestive for our problem about contemporary preference for the spiritual over the gross, and we can try to extrapolate from one to the other.

1 The well-heeled bourgeois elite endowed with both spiritual and economic capital would be expected to support Western traditional medicine. Why not? They are paying for the institutions which issue certification and which are intended to guarantee professional standards. Their judgement confers legitimacy.

2 As to those who have economic but lack symbolic capital, their being untrained in the enjoyments of refined taste might make them less enthusiastic for the spiritual end of the scale. At the least they are ill-

equipped to judge the finer nuances. Some of them will certainly go for more robust choices, and we would not expect them to be candidates for a spiritualized medical theory.

3 The radical critique of the French establishment flourishes among those who are strongest in symbolic capital and weakest in economic resources. We can treat the spiritual critique of modern medicine as parallel to the Left Bank critique of artistic taste. The same conditions that favour the radical critique would provide a sympathetic environment for the spiritual option.

Bourdieu has given us a kind of social epidemiology of where in a certain kind of society we should expect to find the demand for spiritualized medicine. But if we want to do research to test his model the question is how to exit from the tight framework of French culture. We need a more general model of where the taste for spiritual solutions is located. Bourdieu's argument implies that taste is always going to be harnessed to the struggle for hegemony in a particular community. He must be right: although good taste claims to rest on universal principles, it is always challengeable; the challenge comes from those who would subvert the established order, and the struggle is between them and those who want to manipulate it.

If we boldly draw an equivalence between the models of French good taste and Indian ritual purity we can see that in both cases the spirituality index has been harnessed to the social ranking of a hierarchical society, though inversely. For that reason neither case corresponds to what we are witnessing in respect of the demand for gentle solutions. For the movement which we are trying to understand is explicitly egalitarian. It is hostile to domination, and hostile to the authority of Western science. The

contest polarizes two constructions of the medical practitioner, one, whose authority depends on Western science
and on the industrial democracy which produced it, and
the other, who draws his authority from esoteric sources,
from ancient cosmic knowledge.

Between one medical theory and another two views
of reality are at issue. Traditional Western medicine and
complementary therapy teach opposed theories about how
the universe is divided up and where the parts fit together.
We are dealing with two cultures. The question is not how
two different realities become credible, since the reality is
one. The question is about two different medical 'credi-
bilities'. Some form of analysis more distanced, more
abstract and generalizable will be necessary.

Sickness as a resource

To talk fairly about what is credible and incredible in both
forms of medicine the argument has to retreat to a level of
abstraction which includes each as credible. Comparing
two cultures, there can be no shouting down the other side,
no privileging what is credible to one party and down-
grading what is credible to the other. It would be cheating
to take on board bits and pieces of the other view while
rejecting various parts as unacceptable. To proceed by
saying that chiropractice is acceptable but not acupuncture,
aromatherapy but not reflexology, or the other way round,
is merely exerting prejudice. A fair argument needs to be
conducted on a common ground.

The cultural theory that I will apply starts from
questions about solidarity. Culture is the way people live
together. I would like to assume that it is extremely difficult for a group of people to live together in an organized
way without force, and that heavy tactics of persuasion

have always been used when any solidarity appears, even for a short time. Solidarity always needs explaining; long-term social harmony, I assume, is more difficult than short-term. As soon as I have proposed this minimum basis for my argument, I discover that minimal though it is, it does not provide a common ground. My challengers will say that I am horribly biased in assuming that conflict is more probable than harmony; they will maintain that living together is no problem, so long as there is good will, kindness and self-denial.

Immediately our search for a common ground for the argument has to begin again. Can we take it that solidarity is desirable? And admirable when it appears? Is it safe to assume that we can recognize it when it is there? If we can agree that it is sometimes absent, then we may have some common ground for considering the forms of persuasion that produce variety among cultures.

This basis of comparison is fair to both sides. The argument will make the sick Londoner who is choosing complementary medicine equivalent to the African villager who is confronted by the reverse option. The choice is not between science or mumbo-jumbo, but choosing the traditional versus the exotic system, and in effect it means choosing between therapeutic communities. The African patient faced with the choice between the Christian missionary doctor with an exotic pharmacopaeia and the traditional diviner with his familiar repertoire is under the same sort of pressures as a Westerner choosing between traditional and exotic medicine. For minor ailments he can pick and choose separate remedial items without incurring censure, but if it is his own life or the life of his child that is at risk, his therapeutic community will take a strong line. He may have friends on either side of the divide, or choosing may involve him in a complete switch of loyalties. It is rather like religious conversion: if there is a strong political alignment dividing the two therapies, there will be political pressure not to convert to the other side. That is a good beginning for the anthropological approach.

The next step is to follow the monitoring that is going on in any community. Wherever there is illness, warnings are being issued, and informal penalties being threatened. Talcott Parsons founded medical sociology when he identified and named the 'sick role'. When a person defines himself as sick, he can escape censure for doing his work badly, being late, being bad-tempered, and so on, but the community which indulges the sick role also exacts a price: the sick person is excused his remiss behaviour on condition of accepting the role, eating the gruel or whatever is classified as invalid food, taking the medicine, and keeping to the sick room, out of other people's way.

Having adopted the sick role, a person cannot play his or her normally influential part. The patient is reproved for trying to go on working; if the patient complains of pain, the answer is that complaining is aggravating the condition and a more severely restricted diet may have to be prescribed; every complaint is met with potential criticism so that the patient ends by lying back and accepting the way others have defined the sick role. Dragging around looking tired, his friends ask if the doctor has been called in yet, and if so, they want to know who, and are free with advice as to who can be trusted. It is a matter of pride for them if their favourite doctor is called, and a threat of withdrawn sympathy if it is one they disapprove. These friends interacting with the patient, listening to symptoms and offering advice, form what the anthropologist John Janzen (1978) calls the 'therapeutic community'.

At the early stages of illness, there is some choice: either behave as if you are well or admit to being sick and bear the consequences. If the illness worsens and the invalid refuses the advice of friends and family, it is going to be difficult to ask for the neighbourly services or the loans of money on which lying in bed depends. The rival merits of traditional and alternative medicines are put to the test, not according to the patient's recovery but according to the negotiating of the sick role. The outcome will depend on the therapeutic community. For the sick person, the power of the medical theory counts for less than issues of loyalty and mutual dependability, unless he or she is completely isolated.

The background assumption is that any society imposes normative standards on its members. That is what being in society involves. Living in a community means accepting its standards, which means either playing the roles that are approved, or negotiating the acceptability of new ones, or suffering from public disapproval. The option for spirituality is a form of negotiation. But of course communities differ in the amount of control they exert: some are quite lax and standardization is weak; others exert ferocious control. In this perspective it would be interesting to know whether the persons who have chosen alternative therapy have also chosen a therapeutic community to support them with friendship and counsel.

For medical anthropology patterns of accountability are probably the most revealing of all the comparisons that can be made between different medical systems. It stands to reason that the more organization that is being attempted, the tighter the scheduling of coordination and the stronger the controls imposed. Where minutes count, the ambulance arriving half an hour after being called can be disastrous. Living in a tightly coordinated society can itself be a source of strain and when the time factor starts to count more than the personal factor we glimpse a constraining set of circumstances. Bureaucratic mechanisms, lack of human concern, erratic interventions, episodic treatment, over-crowded clinics, unexplained delays would diminish confidence in modern medicine and tempt towards the gentler therapies and their more regularly sustained treatments in the all-embracing cosmic scheme of things. These are the kinds of differences which cultural theory takes into account.

Starting from the idea that blaming and criticizing are essential social processes, anthropology recognizes that medicine is always under community control, and its justifications are always severely scrutinized. It is not just because health, life and death are important in themselves. All sickness and bodily impairment are grounds for demanding justification and so superb material for the blaming and justifying process. In the most extreme form, every illness affords scope for an accusation. If someone is sick, they can be accused of not taking proper care of their bodies. The sick person is not necessarily the one who is accused: if it is the children, the parents are accused, or the school, or the public sanitation. In this context of mutual recrimination the body is a medium for exerting control; pointing to a sick body is a potential threat against anyone who can be held accountable. Doctors do not normally think of sickness as grounds for accusations, and to some this view may be repellent. But we are not doing medicine, we are doing anthropology, and this is the most promising approach for comparing rival constructions of the therapist.

Cordon Sanitaire and handwashing

Medical anthropology has to be interested in the way that health is invoked to promote collaboration and rejection.

36

Theories of contagion, for instance, serve as fences for keeping undesirables out. Leprosy, for example, without any well-founded diagnostic principles, was made a cause for segregating large numbers of the poor and landless in twelfth-century Europe. Bubonic plague was associated with immorality in the fourteenth century and everywhere believed to be brought by foreigners. If there were no danger from plague the people would have found other reasons for restricting travel and trade, but the disease afforded a powerful weapon for self-interested blaming and excluding. Since community always involves judgement and persuasion, the fragile human body is the political touchstone, and blame is the justification for exclusion.

Medicine is there, right in the middle of whatever issues are at stake, because human bodies are always at risk. But different kinds of societies allocate blame in different patterns. Medical anthropology ought to be able to describe these patterns: if the Punjabi patient has a sinking heart, what does he expect his community to do about it? If the Lele with pneumonia suffers from crossed-over ribs, what can be done to uncross them? In either case, what was the initial cause of the ailment? Who is to blame? The patient, or the doctor, or the mother-in-law? We will never get a satisfactory medical anthropology unless we demand to know the whole scenario. It is just not interesting to describe diagnoses, as if they were museum items. We need a holistic context. According to what kind of blaming is going on, so will the role of the therapist be differently constructed, to avert the finger of blame, to point it, or to attract it.

In some communities blame-averting techniques are well developed. Where social patterns are highly competitive and individualistic, no one who is engaged in the race for success will have time or resources to help the less successful. If the rewards for winning are great and the penalties for defeat heavy, failure will penalize the unsuccessful competitor's family as well as himself. In such a system failure is a frightening prospect; one who sees the scales turning against his own efforts will be apt to feel depressed and worried, become listless, lose appetite. His poor health is a reproach to his neighbours, but what can they do? A large loan can hardly be spared to one whose state of health suggests he is a bad risk, and all the introductions to the powerful network are being used for family already. What is needed when it is impossible to cure the sickly neighbour is a ceremony that amounts to a show of sympathy while washing hands of responsibility. There are many examples of handwashing ceremonies.

The Gurage in Ethiopia used to have a theory that these symptoms indicate possession by a hungry spirit. When the friends and neighbours perform this ceremony the evil spirit is supposed to go away satisfied, allowing its victim to recover without further intervention (Shack, 1971). The therapist who plays the role of intermediary between malevolent spirit and human patient expects his fee. Who pays it? If the community is washing its hands of further responsibility, it might be reasonable to expect them to pass the hat round. If the patient does not recover, does he get called in again? Or is he sued for failure?

From the point of view of the community the belief in bad spirits which upholds the handwashing ceremony is relatively harmless, because no human gets blamed. The diagnostic theory sounds harsh, since the rite of exorcism does not help the patient in any of the material ways he needs to be helped. But comparatively it is benign, because neither the patient nor any of his enemies are made to carry the blame for his illness and the therapy enables everyone to get on with their lives.

Elsewhere responsibility for sickness has more sinister repercussions. Someone, neither the victim nor a hungry spirit, may be held responsible for insidious harm. This kind of diagnosis unleashes latent passions of fear and hate, and accusations are liable to tear the community apart. If this is the scene of diagnosis, then the therapist is constructed to point the finger of blame, and will presumably get paid by the accusers. In another type of society, the sick person is held to be suffering in punishment for his own delinquencies. For everyone except the patient this is a form of handwashing in which the patient is made to carry the guilt of sickness. Though certainly unjust, in its social consequences this diagnosis supports the moral code. It is rough on the deviant, and much too kind to the sanctimonious busybody who is ready to suppose that the sick persons brought their troubles on themselves. But it has the great advantage that it lets the neighbours off the hook and does not set them against one another in angry recriminations.

It is tempting to dismiss the blaming and excluding processes of exotic or archaic medical diagnostics on the grounds that they belong to far away times and places. But blaming and excluding go on everywhere, and a medical anthropology that does not recognize this is trivial. The more highly organized the society, the more intense the accusing and inculpation. Modern medicine gives scope for prosecution whenever risks to health are incurred. So do not think that the approach via blaming is only relevant to distant tribes or far off history. The accountability of modern medicine is highly institutionalized and the variation between nations is interesting in itself.

The United States and the United Kingdom are two industrial nations which have inherited and share the same medical system. They can none the less differ in their medical practice according to the kinds of accountability to which the profession is subjected. In England professional accountability used to be high and doctors' first answerability was to the profession. Being struck off the list of accredited practitioners was a professionally exercised control; patients would turn to the British Medical Association for redress before announcing their troubles to the press. In the United States the medical profession which has a powerful political lobby is relatively weak in policing its own members and more responsive to demands for accountability which come from the press and other lobbies. This makes a difference in judging what to do in a crisis. It is a pattern of accountability which makes for a more interventionist medical bias. In response to the media, the medical authorities have to be shown to be 'doing something', and to be more inclined to accept the 'worst case scenario'. For example, when a swine flu epidemic was predicted by Swiss researchers in 1976, the Americans, afraid of public censure, planned nation-wide prophylactic measures in case the worst should befall, while the British, more afraid of looking fools in the eyes of their colleagues and better protected from the media, were more sceptical about the evidence and decided not to undertake a massive inoculation campaign. In the end the worst did not befall and the more cautious policy turned out to be right. But do not think that the doctors were acting on personal insights; their insights were socially constructed by the other institutions to which their patients and colleagues and they themselves subscribed.

Cultural bias

In applying the analysis of accountability to therapists in complementary medicine we are looking at the other end of the spectrum, not at those in positions of professional influence but at the general public making their choices about what kind of practitioner they prefer. To understand their liking for a spiritual medicine we need to set it in the whole context of their other preferences and attitudes to authority, leadership and competition. Cultural conflict is part of the explanation of their choice. We would expect people who show a strong preference for holistic medicine to be negative towards the culture in which the other kind of medicine belongs. If they have made the choice for gentler, more spiritual medicine, they will be making the same choice in other contexts, dietary, ecological as well as medical.

The choice of holistic medicine will not be an isolated preference uncoordinated with other values upheld by the patient. Even labelling it more spiritual and claiming it preferable for that reason, implies a latent protest against an established culture labelled materialist. The adepts need not be very articulate in reproaching modern industrial society for its violence and aggressive wars, they may tacitly disapprove the social inequalities, and the unequal distribution of wealth and income; they may privately deplore the destruction of earlier more egalitarian social forms and cherish the traditions of more peaceful epochs. It is not necessarily an overtly political protest, nor does the person who takes these views need to put them more clearly into words about politics. It is enough that they are saying that they believe that all bodies and their own need a gentle therapy.

Anthropology can contribute to the understanding of movements in popular medicine by introducing the idea of conflicting cultural types. Two basic principles have already been introduced:

1 Accountability as the context of community solidarity.

2 The role of illness in constituting the community.

We can add a third principle:

3 The principle of opposition. If one culture is to stay distinct, it needs to be defined in opposition to other cultures.

The idea is that in all their behaviour persons are continuously engaged in trying to realize an ideal form of community life and trying to persuade one another to make it actual. Little that is done or said is neutral, every aspect of living and all choices are tested in the struggle to make a cultural ideal come true. On this approach each cultural type is in conflict with the others and there is no line to be drawn between symbolic behaviour and the rest. Everything is symbolic and it is all heavily engaged. The same analysis that applies to the choice between religions applies to the choice of foods and of medical methods.

There are four distinct kinds of culture, no one of which can flourish in the conditions predicated for any of the others. The four are drawn on the cultural map in Figure 2.1 and can be quickly indicated by saying that one is based on hierarchical community, and so in favour of formality and compartmentalization; one is based on equality within a group, and so in favour of spontaneity, and free negotiation, and very hostile to other ways of life; one is the competitive culture of individualism; and fourth is the culture of the isolate who prefers to avoid the oppressive controls of the other forms of social life. Any choice which is made in favour of one is at the same time a choice made against the others. The choices are made by the subjects of our study, and it is not our place to let personal preference between alternative ways of living bias the discussion.

The choice between gross and spiritual

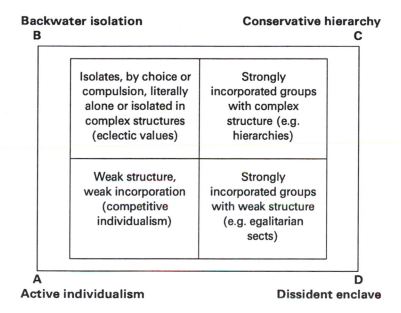

Figure 2.1   *Cultural map*

In the social sciences a choice is treated as an individual matter, arising out of needs inside the individual psyche, and made to satisfy individual needs. The theory of culture, on the contrary, emphasizes the constitution-making capacity of individuals. We assume they are vitally interested in the kind of society they are living in. Any act of choice is also active in their constitution-making interests. A choice is an act of allegiance and a protest against the undesired model of society. On this theory each type of culture is by its nature hostile to the other three cultures. Each has its strengths, and in certain circumstances each culture has advantages over the others. And each has its weaknesses. But all four co-exist in a state of mutual antagonism in any society at all times.

It is important to appreciate that a person cannot for

long belong to two cultures at once. The contradiction will be too difficult to live with, unless the contexts are completely apart, home separated from office, leisure from home, etc. The cultures are in opposition to one another. Certain key preferences denote unambiguous alignment because they cannot be reconciled with their opposite. If the spiritual is chosen the material is ruled out. Formality cannot be practised at the same time as informality. Specialized functions are not compatible with general participation. No one can have both at once. Hierarchy disvalues equality, fervour opposes cool judgement, the excitement of crowds is at odds with the calm of order and the joys of solitude. We can think of more examples of cultural impossibilities: prepared sermons from the pulpit exclude spontaneous witnessing; standing rigidly to attention excludes rolling in the aisles; heterodoxy is opposed to orthodoxy.

Figure 2.2 illustrates in a general way the dynamics of opposed cultural bias. B–D is the diagonal of withdrawal or protest. B classifies persons who have been driven out of the running for power and influence by too strong competition, or who have chosen to keep out of the rat race, to avoid even trying to exert power. B is a backwater by definition. The dissent is private, idiosyncratic, but not necessarily unhappy or angry. D classifies organized dissenting enclaves, usually indignant against the abuse of power and wealth. Religious sects are the most familiar model of the enclave culture. Though there is no expectation that cultural conflict in this corner will always focus on religion, the debate that the enclave engages on principles of governance tends to raise the metaphysical stakes, so the more active the confrontation between the establishment and the enclave the more likely that spiritual values will be invoked sooner or later by the latter.

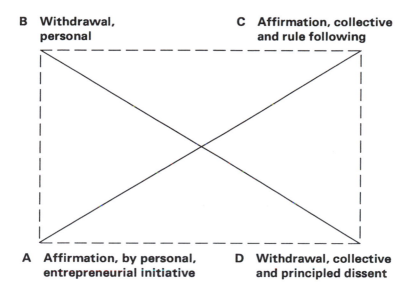

B **Withdrawal,**
personal

C **Affirmation, collective**
and rule following

A **Affirmation, by personal,**
entrepreneurial initiative

D **Withdrawal, collective**
and principled dissent

Figure 2.2   *Diagram of opposed cultural bias. The diagonal*
A–C is the positive diagonal, the alliance of individual
entrepreneurs with hierarchies, affirming authority; the
diagonal B–D is the negative diagonal, the alliance of isolates
with dissident enclavists, rejecting existing authority

The diagram in Figure 2.2 is a technique for thinking
about culture without indulging subjective bias. It explains
how a bundle of preferences can be coded as either at the
spiritual or the material end of the spectrum. The theory is
not deterministic. No one is forced by cultural pressures to
choose one way or another. It does not even assume that
people know what they want, but it does assume that they
know what they do *not* like, and that they are realistic
about their opportunities.

Moving between the different sectors is theoretically
easy. Migrants, refugee victims of persecution or war and
other displaced persons will be candidates for the corner of

the isolates. Historically many enclaves have been formed by disaffected hierarchists. Anyone who has rightly been classed as an isolate may suddenly have the opportunity, for example, to own a street vendor's barrow or otherwise become a small-scale entrepreneur. Should his enterprise turn out well his formerly passive views about the universe will be likely to turn into the opportunism of the individualist culture. Or failing such opportunity, there is nothing to stop a few isolates from banding together and forming an enclave, ethnic, religious, or a therapeutic community. However, practice is different from theory, and in real life it is not always so easy to make the move between cultures, especially if friends see it as betrayal.

The negative diagonal

In any community there will be some sectors which support the structure of authority. They are allies on the positive diagonal (A–C). Both types of cultural ideal accept authority, leadership and domination. Appropriate use of force poses no problem for them; they are much more liable to worry about subversion, arbitrariness and anarchy. By the same token, anything that they approve will automatically be up for question by the cultures on the negative diagonal (B–D). By definition the isolates will not be able to exert influence and will not expect to use force to attain their ends. The enclavists will have combined together in protest against the domination of the mainstream society. Both the cultures on the extremes of the negative diagonal will be fertile ground for protest, and the obvious common ground they have for protest is about the use of power.

For the people on the positive diagonal authority is in principle acceptable; in their different ways they are seeking to exert it; violence is disapproved if it is arbitrary, the subordination of animals is taken for granted. On the positive diagonal the coding of 'spiritual' versus 'material' values is weak. Like everyone else, they will recognize the contrast of spiritual, subtle, pure, refined etc. as distinct from material, gross, impure, vulgar; the coding is going on all around them. It will not be used to refer to power and wealth, but to assess the relative value of work and leisure; commercial values will be coded more 'materialist' compared with ethics and art; spectator sports, boxing, wrestling, football, as less 'refined' enjoyments than literature, music, painting, sculpture. In Pierre Bourdieu's scheme of good taste this unradical, unpolitical coding will be coming from the sections of society who are well endowed with economic capital, ready to maintain and collaborate unproblematically with the social system as it presents itself.

On the other hand, 'spiritual' and 'pure' are more meaningful codings for isolates and enclavists, and for them 'materialist' conveys strong disapproval. They find themselves peripheralized in the mainstream society, unable to exert power, and without influence. On Pierre Bourdieu's scheme these will be the people who tend to be short of economic capital, but though they may not have symbolic capital in the form of education, they will have many ways of appropriating legitimacy to themselves. The preference for the spiritual is a grading and exclusionary device for use as a weapon in the war between cultures.

Set in the larger context which includes Indian vegetarianism and other ancient movements to cherish animal rights, it becomes easier to see why cultural alignments demand to be expressed according to a spirituality index. Wearing furs and eating meat, both of which license violence to animals, would come to symbolize corruption and abuse of privilege. All the products of violence stand at the impure or gross end of the spirituality scale, and would be associated with disregard for the environment and contempt for human values. If we can see how we ourselves develop definitions of pure and gross through classifications of food and clothes, we can see the spiritualist critique of medicine in the same perspective. The diagram of cultural bias shows how the conflict between two medical systems is part of the polarization of the two diagonals. On the negative diagonal where it makes sense to be against harsh controls and exercise of authority, the option for spirituality is the more compelling.

Not everyone whose back is cured by a chiropractor or whose rheumatism is treated by a herbalist is committed to an explicit political programme. At the same time I do not know of any research that has inquired specifically about which sections of the population prefer spiritual versus material values. Colleagues who ask for quantitative evidence of the value of this cultural analysis must admit in fairness that the usual surveys are not made on this basis. They generally are content to draw up their comparisons on the narrow basis of choices between therapies. Or they try to find out if the adepts for holistic medicine are alienated or not. For stratifying the sample of the population used for surveys they use the usual demographic classifications. But political alignment is too gross a test for a subtle inclination to spirituality. And neither demography, nor income, nor education reveal cultural bias.

The movement for gentle therapies is a strong cultural undertow which does not show in answers to questionnaires about political or religious affiliation. We can specify what the kind of research that would test this admittedly speculative approach would need to do. First it would establish the local indicators for the 'spirituality scale'. This would have to be carried through the whole range of choices between gross and subtle, in food, clothing, decor, entertainment and politics. Choices of therapies would be expected to resonate with established cultural bias, and from this the role of the therapist could be predicted.

The argument suggests that holistic, spiritualized medicine is going to be a permanent feature of our cultural landscape. With the spread of industrialization a cultural audit would show that the negative diagonal is well populated. Industrial society tends to draw individuals out of their primordial contexts of loyalty and support and strands them in the sector of the isolates. Where enclaves and isolates flourish the spiritual critique will continue to challenge the definitions of reality given by traditional Western medicine.

References

Bourdieu, P. (1979) *La Distinction*. Paris: Editions Minuit.

Herzlich, C. and Pierret, J. (1985) 'The social construction of the patient: patients and illnesses in other ages', *Social Science and Medicine*, 20(2): 145–51.

Janzen, J. (1978) *In Quest of Therapy in Lower Zaire*. Berkeley: University of California Press.

Krause, Inga-Britt (1989) 'Sinking heart: a Punjabi communication of distress', *Social Science and Medicine*, 29(4).

Marriott, McKim (1976) 'Hindu transactions, diversity without dualism', in Bruce Kapferer (ed.), *Transaction and Meaning: Directions in the Anthropology of Exchange and Symbolic Behaviour*. Philadelphia: ISHI.

Sermeus, G. (1987) *Alternative Medicine in Europe: a Quantitative Comparison of the Use and Knowledge of Alternative Medicine and Patient Profiles in Nine European Countries*. Brussels: Belgian Consumers Association.

Shack, W. (1971) 'Hunger, anxiety and ritual: deprivation and spirit possession among the Gurage of Ethiopia', *Man*, 6(1): 30–43.

3

Bad Taste in Furnishing

Decoration

How can value be grounded now, in a relativist world? My first response is to question whether the world of art is any more divided as to value than it has been at any other time. Take the example of decoration. There is nothing new about the fact that some are fervently in favour, and others as fervently against. My argument will proceed by tracing antipathy and embarrassment. I will develop an anthropological thought, introduced already but taken further in the next chapter, that taste is best understood by negative judgements. The discourse about dislike and ugliness is more revealing than the discourse about aesthetic beauty.

Wherever we lived, when I was a child, our walls were white, well, not quite, a yellowish white called cream. Patterned wallpapers, I would hear them say, were fussy, distracting. The adults who defended their antipathy to decorated walls supported their case by an appeal to nature: patterned walls are actually bad for you. I learned young that a busy pattern could prevent a good night's sleep, and even make a fever worse. Putting a sick person in a room with patterned walls was bad nursing, as every whitewashed hospital room bore witness.

On the other side, the Keeper of Oriental Antiquities at the British Museum starts her book on ornament with a strong attack against bare walls. 'We all know and have always known', she declares in her own appeal to nature, 'that blank surfaces are repellent and test our endurance. Prisoners are confined to bare cells and interrogated in bare rooms where there is no relief to the eye in the forms of lines, let alone ornament, to break the monotony of the white walls' (Rawson, 1984, p. 17). I am grateful to the Keeper, Jessica Rawson,[1] for our talks about ornament and for choosing the pictures of Chinese pottery used here to illustrate the argument. They are pots used at the Chinese court in the eleventh to the twelfth centuries.

First she chose an example of Ding ware, an incense burner made for court use in the late eleventh and early twelfth century (Figure 3.1). She considers that the shape and surface, though white, are 'fussy' and 'ornamental', and she likes it a lot. The fine white porcelain stands on slender feet, like a piece of metal work. The delicate design is in a continuous tradition going back for 200 or 300 years, and indeed, it is based on earlier silver ware from the eighth to the ninth century (Figure 3.2).

But in 1126 there was a political disaster: the Song court was chased out of Northern China by tough nomadic invaders from the North, who captured the emperor, dethroned him, and founded their own new dynasty. The dispossessed Song court took up residence south of Shanghai, and made a fresh start. The new court austerely repudiated the ornamentation of the preceding period and patronized the fashion for green ware. Though requiring immense skill from the potter, it called on more primitive antecedents. It was produced in heavier, plainer styles based on bronze forms of a much earlier dynasty. White pots continued to be used, but seem to have been less prized than the green ones.

The bowl in Figure 3.3 is heavy and plain and although the design is austere, it is elegant enough for use at court.

Figure 3.1 *Ding ware incense burner*

Jessica Rawson draws my attention to the gentle curve and luscious, silky surface. Here is an outright statement against ornament, and in favour of direct tactile qualities.

Also from the twelfth or thirteenth century, and likewise designed for court use, is the incense burner in Figure 3.4, which is also unadorned except for a complex crackle glaze demanding immense skill from the potter to produce the prized antique surface look. Its metal prototype is extremely ancient, c.900 BC, much earlier than the silver prototype of the white ornamented incense burner (see Figure 3.5).

So this is apparently one more story about swings of

Figure 3.2 *The ninth-century form on which the white
Ding ware incense burner was based*

fashion. On the pendulum theory, if the first stage is
decorated, the next must be plain, and the succeeding style
ought to be decorated. In this case there is also a recurring
primitivist trend: the first 'fussy' style traced its legitimacy
back through two or three centuries; the following plain
period had to jump back much further. The trouble with
usual pendulum theories of artistic change is that there is
no principle that regulates the swings. In this case the
swings in design of pots follow the swings of political
fortunes in royal courts. It is a tale of successive waves of
repudiation, and a slow creeping regrowth of ornament.
(Something very similar can be shown for the history of

53

Figure 3.3 *A green ware bowl*

British silver in the seventeenth and eighteenth centuries.) But swings do not account for everything that is going on. Jessica Rawson has shown me another pot of the same period, which was extensively used (Figure 3.6). It has few claims to elegance, either in surface decoration, or in finesse. A heavy base, a heavy rim, thick sides – one would be tempted to say peasant style, but for the very strong glaze. Either the peasant is very rich, or the middle-class owner from the intelligentsia is making an ambiguous statement of disapproval of the rival styles at court.

Pendulum theory offers no reason why plain appeals at one time, and decorated at another. It implies a fatigue or fashion saturation factor which makes the population tired of plain or ornament, but sometimes the fatigue does not set in for thousands of years. In its favour, pendulum theory focuses on antagonism. As I keep saying, hostility is a more interesting basis for theories of taste than some universal principle of envy.

Figure 3.4 *An incense burner with crackle glaze*
Figure 3.5 *A heavy bronze tripod, c.900 BC*

Figure 3.6 *A thick heavy bowl for drinking tea, which became widespread in southern Asia and is fashionable to this day*

Emulation

According to the theory of emulation, the envious lower classes keep copying the upper-class styles, and the upper keep trying to distinguish themselves, so the style for luxuries seeps down. Anthropologist Daniel Miller applies a theory of emulation developed in the 1970s by a socio-linguist, W. Labov (1972, p. 239), to illustrate what would have been happening to the shape and colour of pots in an Indian village if this theory was right (Figure 3.7).

First happiness goes up as design travels down the social scale, then the upper class begins to be unhappy because its designs are no longer distinctive. It adopts a change, to outpace the low-class emulators, and the emulators' happiness goes down, until they gradually catch up again (Miller, 1985, p. 186). In this upstairs/downstairs model of society the goodhearted socio-linguist sadly contemplates the upward yearnings of the lower class, ever frustrated by the downward trajectories of designs. For him the diagram shows how the design of pots is one more way in which the rich and powerful keep the underclass down.

This version of social life considers only individuals foraging in a field of other individuals of higher and lower status. In the pecking order model lateral links are not considered, nor groupings, nor alliance nor patronage. There are no competing solidarities, no patterns of balance; nothing but individual striving to move up or to keep others down.

For his part, Daniel Miller has complicated the picture by recording pottery shapes and colours in an Indian village (Figure 3.8). Red is the top colour for ritual, Brahmins have red pots; high castes have red and buff; low castes and Untouchables have black pots. If it was just colour, Labov's socio-linguistic model would suffice. But the colour coding of pots is complexly correlated with the purity of substances they contain. The substances are engaged in the exchange system of the village. They cannot be mapped simply on to the social chart of relative ritual purity. In the result, an intensely subtle code is evolved.

Milk is ritually the highest ranking form of food; as the first two pots in Figure 3.8 show, the more completely is the pot associated with milk, the rounder its body and the rounder its rim. After milk are ranked pulses and grains, in more angular pots, straighter lines and a straight-sloping rim. Lowest in the ranking is the squat, wide open, angular pot for meat. Impossible and horrible to think of putting food into the wrong pot (Miller, 1985, p. 153).

Hindu villagers are self-consciously scanning who and what they are contacting, in terms of this ritual code. It is not a straight up/down ladder. A lively tussle is going on

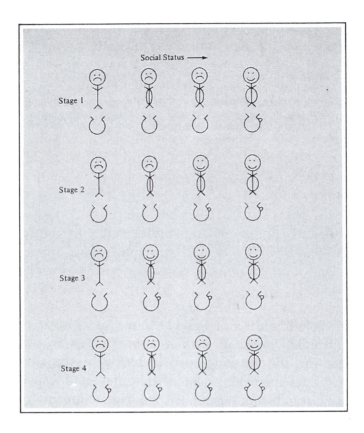

Figure 3.7 *Daniel Miller's happiness principle (Miller, 1985)*

between at least four hierarchies: at the top of the ritual ladder, the Brahmins; at the top of the wealth ladder, the merchants; in control of land and people, the farmers; and the lower castes compete for what they can get. Each is defining his/her relative status and marriage prospects in terms of pots and pans and what food can be given to whom and received from whom (Mayer, 1960).

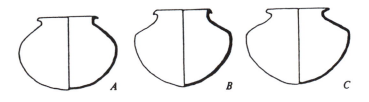

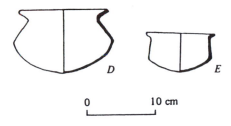

Figure 3.8 *Pot rims and shapes (Miller, 1985)*

The socio-linguist's deplorably thin idea of social inter-action might work in certain communities in certain periods. But for the long span of history a straight up/down model misreads most of the cues, and especially those about gifts and hospitality. Inadequate for the United States, where individualist competition is well represented, it is grotesque for India, where individuals in castes and sub-castes interact with complex rules about food and gifts. Something else beside status envy is at work, something that complicates as it steadies the process.

Does it happen here?

My best friends often complain that my attempts to show the formal nature of taste formation are too mechanistic. They concede I may have a point for foreign parts. But with us, they maintain, it is not so. With us, choice is freer, more personal, more spontaneous; we are modern, so there is more privacy and more choice. To convince you that our tastes also fall into standardized packages (called lifestyles by market researchers), I present here a diagram of living room styles produced by two sociologists in the Chicago area in 1970 (Figure 3.9) (Laumann and House, 1970).

Edward Laumann and James House split the upper/ lower-class ranking of opinion research into two taste groups, traditional and modern. Inevitably this split implies a generation difference as well. In 'traditional style' the high status living room had plain curtains, paintings of scenery, French furniture, books and a piano; also large potted plants. The low status variant had 'translucent curtains' (in England we call them lace or net curtains), floral carpets, religious books abound, as well as photographs and trophies.

The high status 'modern style' had geometric curtains, abstract paintings, modern furniture, an encyclopedia and a hi-fi, and the carpet was not patterned. The low status 'modern style' living room had bulky furniture, floral curtains, animals and religious objects.

One can appreciate that certain choices would be incompatible with others; pets in the living room might threaten the French furniture; the cost of the hi-fi might compete with the cost of the piano. The preference for empty space and an uncluttered feel might work against a taste for large potted plants. Geometric curtains and plain carpets might match up well with abstract paintings and modern furniture. Daniel Miller's diagram of emulatory happiness might show a long slow shift away from net curtains, first towards floral, then to plain, and ending with geometrical in the living rooms of the young high status moderns.

When I talk about this research I generally get a negative

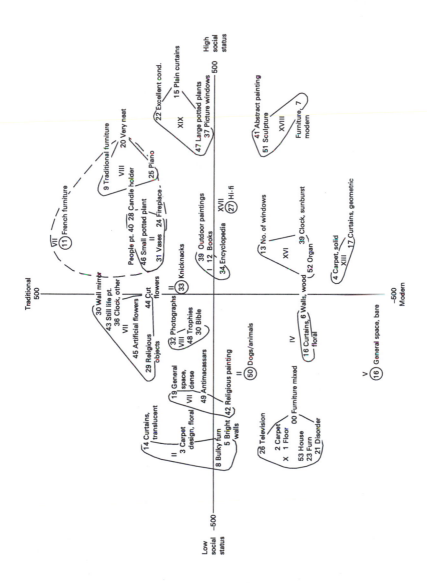

Figure 3.9 *Contrapuntal living rooms (Laumann and House, 1970)*

reaction. 'This is out of date. This is absurd, this is not how I furnish my home, the evidence has been forced; I don't believe it was so predictable.' When it was reported on the television network the authors got strong reactions from the Chicago public, very favourable. Letters poured in; the writers were not complaining of the account, but asking for advice. I never saw the letters, but I imagine them to be like this:

> Dear Dr Laumann, We are about to do over our living room, we are in our fifties, no children . . .

Then the question:

> Are we too old for geometric curtains?

> We are high status, but we have not got the French furniture. Does it matter?

> We are not musical, but should we have a hi-fi for our friends?

Some standardization is evidently going on, but a shift from traditional to modern trends does not account for it. There is competition, but it is polarized across classes. Some hidden process is making streams of colour, pattern and shape pour in from different quarters of the community so that the living rooms appear as correct exemplars of their kind. Two things are needed to make this fascinating research apply beyond Chicago. One is somehow to transcend the names of the objects: somehow we have to go beyond the chairs and curtains to more general categories of classification. The other is to go beyond the assumption that up/down status (measured by wealth and education) predicts taste. Rich or poor, educated or not, you can love floral, or hate geometric, feel your endurance tested to breaking point by plain, or your temperature rise because of decorated walls. The problem is to get at some underlying principle of discrimination.

Potted plants are vying with encyclopedias, pets are being ousted by Louis Quinze reproductions; the scene is too swirling and complex to be described as fashion fatigue; the people too intelligent to be given to simple emulation. A four-sided pattern of conflict explains it better than a one-dimensional up/down status ladder.

Gradation of styles

Think of hostility and rejection:

'I wouldn't be seen dead in it!'
'I wouldn't have it in my house, not if you paid me!'
'No! Never! Across my dead body!'

When you hear (or utter) any of these, you find that the disgusting thing is not badly made, or cheap, or necessarily garish. The cause of the rejection is that the person does not want to be associated with another who would definitely like to be seen with these shoes on, or this tie or scarf.

Gender, age, class, etc., there is plenty of such discrimination at work, and as the signals of contempt are meant to be seen and understood, it should not be difficult to pick them up. A good pot owes its value to its incontestable claim to belong to its own class of pot.

To see what is happening, look at ourselves in everyday life. Like every other culture, ours distinguishes between intimate and public, or between older and younger, upper and lower, insider and outsider. Goods are used to show the distinction between intimate and public, or between older and younger, upper and lower, insider and outsider. The alert fieldworker can observe the whole series of occasions which elicit the gradations between pottery mugs for breakfast, the porcelain cups for tea, and, moving from containers to contents, the instant coffee for the family, the best ground coffee for the guest and so on. The econometricians know how to track the patterning of these choices, and the market researchers rarely miss a beat.

Figures 3.10 and 3.11 show decision trees constructed by Mary Ann Maguire.[2] These diagrams do not display the gradings of an exotic hierarchy like China's, nor a unique ritual complex, like Hinduism. They have been constructed to show how the average American family makes its decisions about food, and we can assume that the decisions about what to eat entail other decisions about pots and cutlery. The best china is not for subgroup O.

Anywhere in the world the scale from gross to refined is in use, though defined in different ways. Consider the range between earth, wood, glass to metals, and start again from aluminium, steel, brass, copper, silver, gold. The same gamut classifies surfaces, natural, rough and all the way to polished, smooth or lacquered. The same scale exists for the subjects of pictures, from bodily functions to formal court scenes or paradise. And it is all engaged again in the selection of appropriate gifts. Another scale is based on weight and volume; another goes from common to rare. There is no limit to the number of different scales for marking the same meanings: light/dark, hard/soft, loud/ quiet, and the contrast between modesty and broad sexual allusion (Lamont and Fournier, eds, 1992).

Bodily behaviour and style of objects and kind of occasion are all mapped upon each other. Subtle gestures, gentle voices, no wild arm-waving, such restrained comportment is projected on to smooth surfaces, soft curves, well equilibrated shapes, and conversely. We know how to read the code, we know what the tail end of the index normally means, and so we know that it is available as a resource for signalling protest against those who prefer the top end. The intimate, daily, common end of the scale, the

Bad taste in furnishing

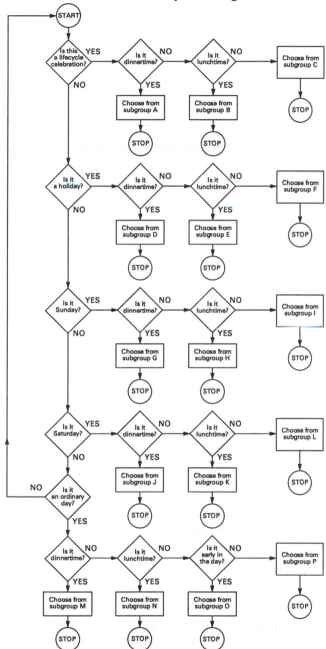

Figure 3.10   *Days and times: housewife's decision tree*

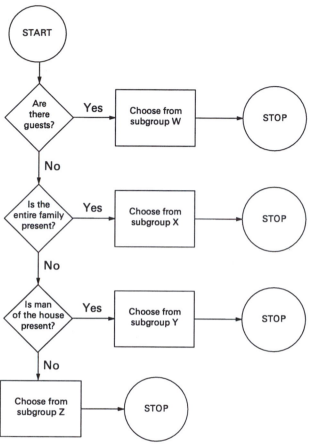

Figure 3.11   *Who will be at the table? Housewife's decision tree*

plain, the small, the unadorned, go straight to the top end of an opposing lifestyle scale. The simple style extols the virtues of the simple way of life.

Instead of looking at separate items, we need to see the whole set of polarized opposites before we can gauge the meaning of one. Instead of individual pots, we should be seeing streams of robustness and saturated colour coming from one direction, and meeting streams of attenuation, lightness and pallor. To know what is happening to taste, we need to trace its manifestations over a whole range of objects, recognizing them as banners in cultural contest.

Cultural theory

As we saw in Chapter 2, cultural theory opposes four types of culture each to the others. First, the most complex, is that where power is backed by authority. The authority tends to be expressed positionally, using spatial contrasts of up and down, right and left. We can expect the positional bias to show on houses, clothes and furniture. Everything is made to display where it belongs in the system of things. The Indian and Chinese ceramics exemplify positional cultures.

But consider the idea of not being seen dead in a certain garment, not accepting a certain kind of object in the house, even if I am paid to have it, and the embarrassment of receiving presents that cannot be displayed because they give the wrong signals. Embarrassment is fear of being wrongly judged, for trying to ape a position one is not entitled to, or resenting someone else for doing just that.

Who ever does follow the herd blindly? Who would accept the dictates of the conservative, positional culture if they did not like it? Or saw nothing for themselves in it? Starting from here we can identify the other three cultural types as revolts against the stifling complacency of the reigning families, their over-subtlety, complexity and over-refinement. We could equally well start from another point on the cultural map in Figure 2.1. The complex culture could as well be shown as a defence against the mess and vulgarity of whatever new wave might be coming, or

against the sanctimonious austerity of the sectarian; and there are those who keep out of the contest and set their own eclectic standards. The diagram of opposed cultural bias from Chapter 2 helps to make sense of cultural conflict, that is, the competing streams of taste and value, and it is worth re-examining it here (see Figure 2.2).

The same range of attitudes to power and authority make the framework for displaying the dynamics of taste. It is like a field of force organized in two dimensions. On the horizontal axis from left to right the individual is more and more deeply committed to a group, and so choices are more standardized as we move from the left across the diagram. The treasured objects likewise will be on the left more adapted to private use, and moving to the right more destined to group celebrations.

On the vertical axis, from bottom to top, the field registers increasing complexity of discriminating rules. The population is spread out over the diagram, some corners more densely populated than others. Those who are living in the culture at the top right-hand corner are creating for themselves a conservative hierarchical structure. The others share a common wish to be distanced from the position-preserving manners and tastes at C.

Call it what you like, complex, conservative, the culture at C makes elaborately graded events to celebrate graded social relations, with graded series of objects in support. Its objects will demonstrate the whole range from gross to refined, inserted into graded spatial and temporal settings, and celebrating the gamut from common to refined. After use, they will be cleaned and put away, resting in graded rows, in graded closets until their time comes round again. A decorated pot, like the Ding ware incense burner, will appear against a complex background of other objects, tapestries and screens.

Over and against all of this, one of the actively opposing cultures will be led by the equivalent of merchant princes, or even brigands or robber barons: as seen from C, they are upstart contenders for power without legitimacy. Call their culture A (acquisitive, aggressive, action-oriented, *arriviste*), their use of objects is quite different. For one thing, the likely absence of lineage implies that their possessions have not been acquired by generations of correct inheritance. Objects are for giving and receiving, for betokening loyalty. They are not worked into the calendar or cycle of seasons, since gestures of alliance may be needed at any time. The objects acquired in these ways cannot be inserted into orderly series. Treasured objects will need to show their value singly, without help from the rest of a series, so they will be impressively heavy, large and durable. The reproach of vulgarity would never bother their owners.

Equally opposed to the acquisitive A and the complex C is the culture of dissidence at D. Here they reject both the inequalities of the complex hierarchy, its grandeur and extravagance, and they also reject the vulgar display of personal power at the other end. The dissident's idea of the good pot comes at the lowly end of the gross–refined scale: unworked finish, simple design, bare of ornament. Its preference for the small end of the scale is a protest against power.

The isolates at B are bypassed by authority and power, for whatever reason; they are not in the game. Failed officials, political exiles, artists, marginals, a diverse set could be located in the backwater. They could be rich. Whether rich or not, they are not usually ostentatious, their possessions are not for display. Backwater taste, though haphazard and heterogeneous, is not developed for seeking favours or for setting standards, attracting followers, or marking big occasions. The concept of the right style is not an issue. They are not going round saying they wouldn't be seen dead, or offended at the wrong style of gift. It would be difficult for a collector to identify an object as corresponding to such an eclectic taste.

Culture is a contest about decoration as much as about anything else. No wonder that some people dislike it as an offence against nature, and no wonder others are passionately devoted to it and consider it a demand of nature. Oversimplifying again, the conservative culture with episodic support from the backwaters would agree that blank surfaces are repellent. The other two hate decoration and like blank surfaces. The active entrepreneurial culture needs to brush aside the formal trappings of the currently established regime, so those people are not against all decoration so much as against that which they regard as effete and overloaded, the style currently preferred by the present hierarchy. They need space for their innovative lives and are against irrelevant clutter.

Embarrassment

Art historians, even if they are not relying on swings of the pendulum, usually give us the chronological sequence of styles. One style comes after and in reaction against the other, and then, the next. I rarely hear from them an account of the synchronic antagonisms, or the attempts to compromise.

The reaction of Reformation styles against Catholic hegemony has given some brilliant exemplars. For example, Michael Baxandall's book (1980) on the limewood sculptures of German churches shows a different sensibility emerging, and a new attention to personality, new materials and new subjects for the expression of individual piety and divine compassion. History assumes that being cut off from sources of marble the sculptors were forced to find another material and so they fortunately hit upon the extraordinary capabilities of limewood. But Baxandall's essay suggests that the shift from grand marble to humble wood, and the demonstration of what a high style wood can achieve, were additional satisfactions. The basic idea was religious reform.

Holland's seventeenth-century style illustrates better the implications of the scale of refinement. First under the yoke of Catholic Spain, then rejoicing in liberty, and then becoming enormously rich, their economic success pro-duced for the Netherlands a cultural problem: how to consume and display great wealth conspicuously without betraying the austere religious codes of Protestantism. Simon Schama (1988) conveys the tension and excitement of a sober style: sombre shining black, with lashings of lace, everything cleaner than imaginable. The burghers got over their embarrassment of riches when they found a way of saying two things at once: the costly display says that they are rich and powerful, whiter than white shows they are refined. The word has become almost unmentionable, yet the embarrassment of vulgarity should not be left unmentioned in the study of good taste.

One of the objections of art historians to the approaches of anthropology and sociology is that we oversimplify. Yes, we do. In real life disputes about taste are passionate; most objects designed to lead a new style are saying more than one thing. The possibility of giving complex messages about loyalty and ambition makes ceramics and other objects so interesting to their owners. Art historians also simplify. By skirting round the problems of cultural con-flict they remove from their discourse the prime question about taste: the origins of vulgarity. They find us embar-rassing, we, the anthropologists. They suspect that our crude imputations of motive do violence to the aesthetic issues. We are hamfisted and unconvincing, easy to put down because we do not know the field. If only a few more historians would join the enterprise, historians who know their period really well, and can track the current feuds and factions embroiled around the exercise of power, we would share a more interesting conversation.

Consider the Amish as a dissenting group, consider the Irish as a backwater of a universal church, a rebel society against imperial Britain. Consider how their popular domestic art depicts their antagonism to the other worlds. Amish furniture is simple, like their way of life, always made of wood, never upholstered. The brilliance of Amish quilts is a surprise. The pieces they are composed from must be unpatterned, the sombre colours are enhanced by bright inserts. Furniture and quilts are made to state the simplicity of their way of life and the vitality and strength of their belief (Bishop and Safender, 1976). This is a classic sectarian enclave, consciously expressing the whole religion in everything it makes.

Consider by contrast the decorated surfaces of Celtic things, the twisted runic designs on antique grave stones. In Ireland see the ancient twisted patterns continued in the design of Irish lace, and recognize its influence in the creamy coloured knitted Aran sweaters. How well it pairs with the highly glazed Belleek china, with its scallopy rims and raised surface decoration. Among the cream coloured tea cups and the dishes of cream sponges and scones, laid out on the creamy linen table cloth, all is enclosed in creamy lace curtains: the squat Belleek teapot flaunts a refined rebuke to the other Irish culture, the Protestant Ascendancy and their friends in the big house, sipping whiskey from refined Waterford crystal. What is all this hyper-refinement for? Unlike the Amish styles it has nothing directly to do with religion. But it might be saying something defiant to English conquerors who liked to call the Irish dirty.

Returning to the pot styles of the twelfth-century Chinese court, the first incense burner we saw, the white Ding ware, would be too ornate for the court that had suffered the embarrassment of surviving the great up-heaval: still ruling, and still rich, they could face out the continuing criticism of decadence by abstaining from frivolously decorated white ware. In an intricate move from complex to simple they preferred to drink from the beautifully refined plain Southern Celadon green ware. Recall that the old northern court, favouring the delicate decorated white ware, had been regularly blamed for decadence and corruption. Their successor, the Song court of the south, adopted a more robust style, undecorated, but so fine that it demanded immense skill to make. The green Celadon ware was helping the new court to say contra-dictory things about itself: we are virile, honest, direct, so we do not like fussy surface decoration, and at the same time, we are intensely refined, witness this pot, the perfect integrity of its form, the thinness of its walls, its perfect balance, its inimitably pure, pale colour. The elaborate decorated white porcelain of the previous era continued to be made and used, but would have given a reactionary political message. I suppose that the loyal supporters of the former regime would have continued to defy the label 'decadent', and flaunted their preference for decorated white ceramics.

And presumably the inveterate critics of court life, accusing both styles of embodying corrupt values, would have had to find a different kind of pot to express their antagonism to pomp, and power. Twelfth-century potters in southern China found the right formula: combining a folksy shape and an opulent glaze, the black, heavy

Temmoku bowl was destined to wide popularity over southern Asia. It seems to be no accident that it was found buried in a scholar's grave, along with his pen and inkstand and other signs of his profession. Could this be the only kind of pot which the privileged but discontented critics of the court could use without undermining what they were saying about fashionable politico-aesthetic values? The pot's heaviness imputes frivolity both to its rivals, the Celadon green ware and the white porcelain, while its shining glaze admits collusion with the general system. Do we have here an early manifestation of the Arts and Crafts movement? These objects are saying several things at once, but what they say can only be known by setting them in their range of similars and opposites.

The sociological project itself is a major source of embarrassment lying between us and the art historians. There seems to be offence, something of a sneer, in pointing out that a thing is not quite what it seems, as if it should not have complex and multiple pretensions. The implicit idea of the art historian who objects to an anthropology of art is that objects are spontaneously what they are, no more, no less; truth requires plain speaking and no ambiguity. If this is not a declaration of taste (which it certainly sounds like), it is saying that art is art and not to be reduced to something else. I take it to be an expression of embarrassment. It says that it is all very well to examine the fine distinctions between pots in ancient China or rural India, and between curtains in Chicago, and to speculate on what pretensions they convey; it is embarrassing to have the pretensions of our own living room brought under the same scrutiny. But embarrassment in itself is as interesting as vulgarity.

In his study of Keats, Christopher Ricks (1974) draws attention to the poet's sympathy for the act of blushing.

Under his subtle touch, embarrassment is elevated to the ranks of the most distinctively human and humane emotions. To be unembarrassable is to be devoid of sensibility and unfit for social life. Embarrassment is a sign that the self is deeply engaged (and is not that right and proper in itself?). It is the sense of disparity between what ought to be and what is there; it is the fear of seeming to be what one is not, of being seen to strive to be more than one should, or less. So complicated are the turns of embarrassment that it makes a person uncomfortably aware of seeing how he seems to others, and even of seeing that they see that he sees. The whole artistic enterprise is engaged, as the poet confronts the immensity of his vision and the poverty of his means. Essentially embarrassment is the response to judgement, and depends on the capacity to judge.

How I wish the historians were less embarrassable: they would not make hidden value judgements. Anthropology is stricter about declaring interest: we allow ourselves to discern the strivings to produce art, but not to pretend to a judgement of value that is beyond the strife. Without more help from uninhibited historians the best I can contribute, as a social anthropologist, to the discussion of value is the chart for mapping the order of battle.

Notes

1 The Keeper at the time of writing, she is now Warden of Merton College, Oxford.

2 I am grateful to Mary Ann Maguire for permission to reproduce these diagrams which she devised while at the Kellog School of Management in Evanston, IL.

References

Baxandall, M. (1980) *The Limewood Sculptors of Renaissance Germany*. New Haven, CT and London: Yale University Press.

Bishop, R. and Safender, E. (1976) *A Gallery of Amish Quilts*. New York: Dutton.

Labov, W. (1972) *Sociolinguistic Patterns*. Oxford: Basil Blackwell.

Lamont, Michèle and Fournier, Marcel (eds) (1992) *Cultivating Differences, Symbolic Boundaries and the Making of Inequality*. Chicago, IL: University of Chicago Press.

Laumann, E. and House, J. (1970) 'Living room styles and social attributes: the patterning of material artefacts in a modern urban community', *Sociology and Social Research*, 54: 3.

Mayer, A.C. (1960) *Caste and Kinship in Central India: a Village and Its Region*. Berkeley, CA: University of California Press.

Miller, D. (1985) *Artefacts as Categories: a Study of Ceramic Variability in Central India*. Cambridge: Cambridge University Press.

Rawson, Jessica (1984) *Chinese Ornament*. London: British Museum Publications.

Ricks, C. (1974) *Keats and Embarrassment*. Oxford: Oxford University Press.

Schama, Simon (1988) *Embarrassment of Riches, an Interpretation of Dutch Culture in the Golden Age*. Berkeley, CA: University of California Press.

4

On Not Being Seen Dead: Shopping as Protest

Shopping

Shopping needs to be explained. Particularly women's shopping needs to be defended, the time they take over it, and the amount of money they spend on it. The ideas that men have about shopping as an activity need rebuttal along with a consumer theory that demeans consumer choice. To make the counter attack I will mention some well-known weaknesses of consumer theory, which is, after all, a one-sided theoretical approach to shopping with crashingly obvious limitations.

Economics and market research are good at explaining the influence of the market on consumers' choices. The basis for that achievement was laid in the nineteenth century with the theory of utility. But nowadays the really difficult problem is the other way round. We need to understand the influence of the consumer on the market. To approach the current question, the effect of the consumers' tastes on markets, the idea of the consumer has to be re-examined. How homogeneous is the consumer's choice? Or, how superficial? How episodic and disconnected from her deeper interests? Why do we suppose that she has any deeper interests than shopping? The very questions, as formulated within the current psychological paradigms, are surprisingly insulting to the intelligence of the shopper, who is, after all, the sovereign rational consumer.

One popular explanation presents the shopper as essentially reactive: she reacts to swings in fashion even more than she reacts to market prices. Swings and prices are the two explanations of shopping: by implication, if the shopper's actions are determined by market or fashion the decisions are mechanical, not worth further examination. There is a respectable literature on hem-lines in this vein. Let us turn to the historic case of Edwardian trouser legs, getting narrower and narrower and then suddenly widening. An apocryphal story favoured in the retail market is that the Prince of Wales, before he became King Edward VII, fell one day into a pond and ruined his trousers: he was forced for the only time in his life to buy a ready-made pair. This did not fit the royal leg so well as those produced by the Court tailor. The politeness of courtiers made loose trousers the height of fashion. The prince's mishap provided the occasion for a swing that was bound to happen anyway. The tube-like Edwardian fashion was facing a point of no return as the tube got narrower and narrower. Eventually the boundary between trousers and hosiery would have to go under (to the professional loss of tailors), or trousers would have to get wider. 'Never trust a man in baggy trousers,' my father was warned by his aged Cambridge tutor. If he thought to arrest a trend, the tutor was wildly optimistic, Oxford bags were to win the day; and now drain pipes have had another turn.

If there is a pendulum, it is going to swing, first one way and then another. But what kind of explanation is it that predicts change but cannot say when or what the change will be? Not everything changes, some fashions stay stable for many generations. Swings of the pendulum have not affected the design of standard knives and forks, used on standard tables on standard plates. It takes an antiquarian expertise to date them. Other civilizations eat elegantly without either knives or forks, Ethiopian, Indian. Why has their pendulum not swung our way in the matter of forks, or why have we not swung into an anti-fork mode? The fact is that swings theory explains very little.

Its supporters qualify it by claiming that only certain choices are subject to swings. The explanation works with an implicit division between purchases based on rational choice, and an optional element, for example, everyone might need a coat, but the colour is optional and liable to swings towards the colour of the year. The implication is that some choices are central and steady, others are peripheral and transient, some have to do with internal, others with external matters, some are about necessaries, others about luxuries or surface decoration. Without some such division between choices, the swings model of the consumer would be absurd.

Style

A contrast of intrinsic/extrinsic features saves swings theory and is congenial to a widely accepted idea of style as *how* a work is done, as distinct from *what* it is. This theory of style implies some essence which can be separated from its appearance: the style is the external surface of a work of art, the polished smoothness or the rough graininess, the surface, extrinsic to the work itself. The theory stops further analysis by the implicit notion that everything has a hidden essence. There is always a reality which the appearance of the thing does not immediately reveal, something inaccessible. This aesthetic philosophy has been thoroughly denounced by Nelson Goodman (1978). If it is misleading in art history, it is pernicious in the theory of consumption. It encourages us to wave away possible reasons for consumer behaviour, wave them away as inherently unknowable. Always be wary of a model of the human mind which brackets off large areas as irrational or unknowable: the conversation-stopper is also a thought-stopper. Ask instead the common-sense question: Why should people adopt a style that has nothing to do with their innermost being? Or, how could a person restrain his inmost being from influencing his regular choices? Or, ask what determines the part of human behaviour that belongs to the irrational periphery? What is the part that belongs to the ineffable inner centre? Consumer theory needs either to answer these questions, or to improve its idea of the human being. This improvement, I suggest, can be made by taking seriously culture as the arbiter of taste.

Market forces go some way to reinforce the swings model by identifying certain parts of consumer behaviour as more responsive to prices than free to follow styles. Changes in technology, new openings for labour, changes in production, these all produce price changes to which the consumer is more sensitive than to fashion. The Post Code code, for example, reveals the lifestyle of the consumer because choice of location responds to a set of market constraints. A given locality affords multiple opportunities connected with the engagement of the householder in the labour market. On the consumption side, if an urban area is so densely populated that there are no gardens, then there will be no call for lawn mowers, pesticides, garden furniture, hoses or sprinklers. A huge bundle of choices tied to the Post Code code are made coherent by reference to market forces. But there are ups and downs of taste which cannot be accounted for by market changes. Even swings theory cannot explain a recent change in attitude to pesticides. It is part of a cultural change, whatever that is.

We have identified some things that are wrong with present paradigms of consumption. It is wrong to suppose that some choices, because they are not obviously responsive to the market, are trivial. It is equally wrong not to take account of the responsiveness of market forces to consumer choice. Above all, it is wrong to consider the consumer as an incoherent, fragmentary being, a person divided in her purposes and barely responsible for her decisions, dominated by reaction to prices on the one hand, and to fashionable swings on the other. Does she have no integrating purposes of her own?

Protest

I argue that protest is the aspect of consumption which reveals the consumer as a coherent, rational being. Though intergenerational hostility is important, consumption is not governed by a pattern of swings between generations. Even between generations, consumption is governed by protest in a much more profound and interesting way. Protest is a fundamental cultural stance. One culture accuses others, at all times. Instead of the weak notion that some choices among consumer goods are acts of defiance, I would maintain much more strongly that consumption behaviour is continuously and pervasively inspired by cultural hostility. This argument will reinstate the good sense and integrity of the consumer.

We have to make a radical shift away from thinking about consumption as a manifestation of individual choices. Culture itself is the result of myriads of individual choices, not primarily between commodities but between kinds of relationships. The basic choice that a rational individual has to make is the choice about what kind of society to live in. According to that choice, the rest follows. Artefacts are selected to demonstrate the choice. Food is eaten, clothes are worn, cinema, books, music, holidays, all the rest are choices that conform with the initial choice for a form of society. Commodities are chosen because they are not neutral; they are chosen because they would not be tolerated in the rejected forms of society and are therefore permissible in the preferred form. Hostility is implicit in their selection.

'I can't stand that ghastly orange colour on the walls,' says the unhappy tenant of a public housing unit (Miller, 1991). She knows perfectly well that a neighbour appreciates that vivid orange colour for its brightness. The colour is implicated in her neighbour's lifestyle. Why does she not paint it over, a decent creamy beige? The anthropologist thinks that she does nothing to remove the thing she hates because she is alienated from the council estate she lives in. Yes, and it might be a positive value for her to have a colour on the wall that she considers ghastly, a reminder of the war against the others and their despised way of life, on behalf of herself and hers. What colours did she wear? No shopper himself, the anthropologist does not report on her other antipathies.

'I wouldn't be seen dead in it,' says a shopper, rejecting a garment that someone else would choose for the very reasons that she dislikes it. The hated garment, like the hair style and the shoes, like the cosmetics, the soap and toothpaste and the colours, signals cultural affiliation. Because some would choose, others must reject. Shopping is reactive, true, but at the same time it is positive. It is assertive, it announces allegiance. That is why it takes so much deliberation and so much time, and why women have to be so conscientious about it, and why it gives them so much satisfaction. That is why men are wise to leave shopping to their wives. Anyway, men's clothing and hair style is much more highly prescribed by the occupational structures in which they spend so much of their lives; they are not sensitized to such a wide diversity of signals. And the fact that men stand outside these arenas of cultural contest explains why they are surprised that things are so costly and why it is difficult to explain to them that so much is at stake. At the beginning of Utility theory there were alleged preferences, then there was the indifference schedule. What has been missing all along is a scale of hostility between cultures. Inquiries about consumption patterns have focused on wants. The questions have been about why people want what they buy. Whereas, most shoppers will agree, people do not know what they want, but they are very clear about what they do not want. Men, as well as women, are adamant about what they do not want. To understand shopping practices we need to trace standardized hates, which are much more constant and more revealing than desires.

Four cultural types

Cultural theory can explain how hates get to be standardized. It assumes four distinctive ways of organizing; four cultures which are each in conflict with the others. Choosing commodities is choosing between cultures, choosing one and rejecting the others. The four types have already been detailed in previous chapters. One is an individualist lifestyle, driving in the fast lane, as the advertisements say. It is a choice for a competitive, wide-flung, open network, enjoying high-tech instruments, sporty, arty, risky styles of entertainment, and freedom to change commitments. In choosing this, the individualists reject the three other styles. One of these is the hierarchical lifestyle, formal, adhering to established traditions and established institutions; maintaining a defined network of family and old friends. (This is definitely driving in the slow lane: it only seems to be a thriftier lifestyle, it costs a lot to maintain the family network, so there is not much cash left for the high-tech, travel, entertainment and so on.) The other lifestyle rejected both by the individualists and the hierarchists is egalitarian, enclavist, against formality, pomp and artifice, rejecting authoritarian institutions, preferring simplicity, frankness, intimate friendship and spiritual values. Finally, there is a fourth type of culture recognized by cultural theory, the eclectic, withdrawn but unpredictable lifestyle of the isolate. Whatever form it takes, it escapes the chores of friendship and the costs imposed by the other types of culture. The isolate is not imposed upon by friends, his time is not wasted by ceremony, he is not hassled by competition; he is not burdened by the obligatory gifts required in the other lifestyles, nor irked by tight scheduling: he is free. Or you could say, in another frame of reference, that he is alienated.

Anthropologists have been interested in cultural strategies as a defence against the possibility of alienation.[1] This argument is on the same lines; there is a defensive element, also an element of attack, not against alienation necessarily, but against the rejected cultural forms. Alienation from one culture does not necessarily leave a person stranded, there are other cultural options. The option for Punk or other subcultures is a rejection of the mainstream cultures, true enough, but rather than an opting out of culture as such, it is a creative cultural strategy in its own right. An isolate is not necessarily alienated in a general way, he can be quite benign in his attitudes to the cultures he does not want to adopt.

None of these four lifestyles (individualist, hierarchical, enclave, isolate) is new to students of consumer behaviour. What may be new and unacceptable is the point that these are the only four distinctive lifestyles to be taken into

84

account, and the other point, that each is set up in competition with the others. Mutual hostility is the force that accounts for their stability. These four distinct life-styles persist because they rest on incompatible organiz-ational principles. Each culture is a way of organizing; each is predatory on the others for time and space and resources. It is hard for them to co-exist peacefully, and yet they must, for the survival of each is the guarantee of the survival of the others. Hostility keeps them going.

Let me pause to illustrate the inherent conflict between cultures. Consumption has been defined by the image of the household shopping basket. Whatever comes home from the shops is designated for use in specific spaces and times. The fast-lane individualist culture is driven by the principle that each person should expand his/her network of alliances. It is hard to do this in a hierarchical household without tearing up the fences and intruding into the reserved times and spaces needful for the hierarchist's lifestyle. The hierarchical and individualist principles are at war, each contemptuous of the other, each seizing a victory where it can. This basic incompatibility lies behind the conflict between generations, and especially between mother-in-law and daughter-in-law, since there is a move-ment towards hierarchy with advancing age. It would not suit either the hierarchist nor the individualist to have the household turned into an egalitarian commune. The isolate tries to avoid alignment, and in doing so gives offence to all, for it is difficult to back out of the cultural conflict going on in any home.

The myths of nature

Anyone hearing this can recognize it, and anyone can see that if there is a constant pressure to define allegiance to

85

one or another of these four conflicting cultures, it will go a long way to explain shopping. But so far it sounds didactic and a priori. The theory is that cultural allegiance pervades all behaviour, including shopping. The consumer wandering round the shops is actualizing a philosophy of life, or rather, one of four philosophies, or four cultures. The cultural bias brings politics and religion into its embrace, aesthetics, morals, friendship, food and hygiene. According to the theory in its strongest version the idea of the consumer as weak-minded and easily prevailed upon is absurd. Only consider the turning away from pesticides, and the turning away from aerosols, artificial fertilizers and carnivorous diets, and consider the great interest shown in the source of energy, whether powered by nuclear, or by solar, or fossil fuels. These examples of consumer preferences are not responses to market conditions. Quite the contrary, they bid fair to change markets profoundly. The consumer has become interested in the environment. But this interest is not uniform. The consumers are found in all four cultural corners: some are in favour of cheap fuel, including nuclear power; others are against it and focus more upon conservation of energy; others simply do not care.

Michael Thompson has led the way in applying cultural theory to the confused and stormy debates on environmental policy (Schwarz and Thompson, 1990; Thompson, 1988; Thompson et al., 1986). In what follows I attempt to apply his method to consumer theory. Thompson's method is to hearken attentively to the debates on the environment and to extract the basic assumptions from their arguments. Infinite regress reaches no conclusion. Eventually explanations must come to an end. Thompson hears the different strands in the environmental debates making appeal to the way that nature is. Nature, being this way or that, can only support this policy, or that, and ruin will follow inexorably on failure to recognize what nature is like. He tracks down four distinctive myths of nature (Thompson et al., 1990). Each is the account of the world that will justify the way of life to which the speaker is committed. The commitment is not a private intention. It is part of the culture with which the speaker has chosen to be aligned. Thompson illustrates the four myths of nature with four diagrams from equilibrium mechanics (Figure 4.1).

A Nature is robust. This version justifies the entrepreneur who will not brook his plans being blocked by warnings that carbon dioxide pollution or soil erosion may cause irreversible damage. His cultural alignment is to a way of life based on free bidding and bargaining. He needs nature to be robust to refute the arguments of those who are against the transactions he has in mind.

B Nature is unpredictable. There is no telling how events may turn out. This version justifies the non-alignment of the isolate. He uses it as his answer to attempts to recruit him to any cause.

C Nature is robust, but only within limits. This is the version that issues from the hierarchists' platform, their justification for instituting controls and planned projects. The hierarchist wants to manage the environment. To justify imposing regulation on the entrepreneur's projects he needs nature to be not completely robust.

D Nature is fragile and pollution can be lethal. This position is entered in fundamental disagreement with the policies of development entrepreneurs and with organizing hierarchists, and with the fatalism of the isolate. It is the version that justifies the anxiety of the green lobbies.

Cultural theory starts by identifying the context of

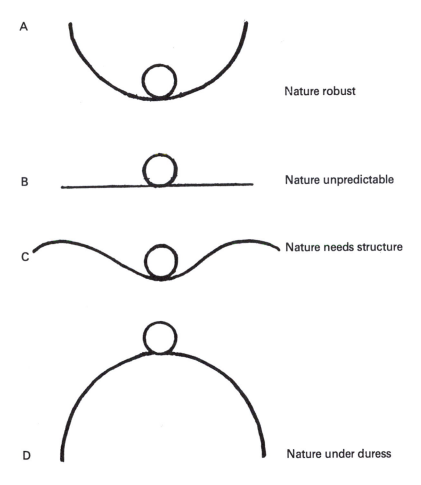

A — Nature robust

B — Nature unpredictable

C — Nature needs structure

D — Nature under duress

Figure 4.1   *Myths of nature (Schwarz and Thompson, 1990)*

appeals to nature, then it uncovers the strategies of debate, and shows the foundation myth as the final clinching argument. In fact, the base line does not clinch anything, because there is no way of demonstrating that one or the

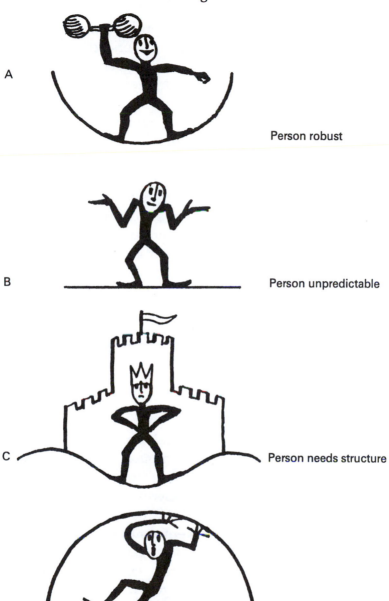

Figure 4.2   *Myths of persons (drawn by Pat Novy)*

other myth of nature is the right one. At some point the summoning of evidence becomes unnecessary; more evidence will not settle the divergence of opinion. Somewhere along the line the debaters realize that they are facing infinite regress, more explanations calling forth more counter-explanations, and when this happens, theorizing has to end. In a debate about what to do with the environment, explanations come to rest on their appropriate myths of nature. The task of cultural theory is to decompose the elements of the argument, and show how each vision of nature derives from a distinctive vision of society, individualist, isolated, hierarchical, or egalitarian. If the debaters were to take up their issues from the vision of society, instead of from its justification, they would confront the choice between organizing principles, instead of vilifying one another for moral obloquy. Between visions of society there is no moral judgement. We are dealing in preferences, assessments of the outside conditions, aptitudes for achieving different kinds of results.

Myths of persons

With a little ingenuity this cultural analysis can be turned around so as to apply to consumption. First, the field of shopping is not the global scene of disappearing forests, eroded soils, or large-scale desertification. The field is defined by the shopping basket. The arguments are not about how to persuade governments or control multinational companies, but how to organize the household. We will hear an argument going on, and there will be recurring clinching phrases, and regular appeals to nature. But of course these foundation myths do not refer to the nature of the physical environment. In the contest about shopping the threat of infinite regress is blocked by reference to the nature of the person. The choices relate again to regulation and control, but this time to regulation of persons, not of the environment. Let us take each of the myths of nature in turn and extrapolate from them what the corresponding myths of the person would be (Figure 4.2, p. 89).

Whoever wants to claim that nature is robust enough to take any amount of knocking about is using nature to defend the entrepreneurs' claim to do the knocking about. We would expect that claim to be paralleled in the case of the person on whom that householder wishes to put constraints. The entrepreneur householder will claim that the nature of the person is very robust so long as it is not put under stifling controls; the person's true nature is to be free and will suffer damage if constrained.

As to the isolate, with no reason for sustaining any particular view of the natural environment, neither would he have reasons for a sustained view of the nature of the person. The way of life of the household isolate is maintained by an uninvolved eclecticism. On the other hand, the hierarchist, whose way of life is to organize and be organized and whose justification is that the environment can only be safe if it is regulated, will argue that it is the nature of the person to thrive within organizations. Structure is a support, a necessary support for the person. Lastly, whoever disagrees with all of these outlooks because of commitment to an egalitarian social order, will have the same argument for the nature of the person as for the nature of the biosphere. The same corrupt, unequal structures that have caused the pollution of the environment will also contaminate the child.

The source of foundation myths of nature also produces foundational models of persons justifying or rejecting claims of authority from other persons. If these four models of the person are sound they deliver the consumer from the reproach of superficial, fashion proneness. It is cultural competition that causes the underlying coherence of consumption choices. Cultural competition is a matter of conscience. Looking for coherence from the point of view of individual psychology will never reveal the conscientious shopper defending a cultural outpost. Psychology has no idea of what she might be protesting against. But according to cultural theory, when she chooses a commodity she chooses a flag to wave and she knows who she is waving it against. Her front door is a public show, to encourage fainthearted followers: she may want them to stay loyal and keep cleaning, or to break out of the chains and leave the step alone: either way, the step is a sign. The choices are acts of defiance, intimidation and persuasion. Buying groceries or cosmetics is buying weapons. Tables and chairs, detergents and polishes are badges of allegiance. Choosing pots and pans or pharmaceuticals is declaring dogma. So far from being mindless, shopping demands infinite attention. Pressed hard by enemy forces, it calls for constant vigilance, subtlety, and resource.

Occupational opportunities

The argument about cultural hostility has, until recently, lacked facts to support it. The statistics of consumption have been collected within an interpretive framework based on individualist psychology. For a long time no empirical research was designed to test cultural theory. Now, however, that has changed. First there was the work of Gerald and Valerie Mars on the cultural alignment of London households. Then there was the re-analysis of survey data by Aaron Wildavsky and Karl Dake (1990) which connected attitudes to risk to political preferences.

Now there is the new research being conducted by Karl Dake, Aaron Wildavsky and Michael Thompson on 'energy futures' and consumption patterns.

The upshot is that cultural alignment is the strongest predictor of preferences in a wide variety of fields. The shopper's sanity has been vindicated. Her integrity is no more in doubt. She shows far more coherence and stead-fastness than under the reigning idea of consumers react-ing to market opportunities and fashion swings. She is revealed in her power, the main arbiter of the demand to which the market responds, before whose sovereign judgements the market stands in awe.

In *Cheats at Work* (1982), a study of occupational crime, Gerald Mars has identified different cultural types in the workplaces of modern industrial society. The social environment, being dominated by large-scale hierarchical organizations, exemplifies distant authority, centralized and delegated. Within its interstices there is scope for workers bonding together in ranked hierarchical units working for their own interest, also scope for egalitarian groups bonded for the sharing of some common booty, and scope for isolates and entrepreneurs working on their own. Systematizing, he finds the four types indicated by cultural theory:

1 Individualists can be recognized as lone operators, working for themselves; specially favourable conditions are prepared for them by remote hierarchical control. Where incentives have been sucked out of institutions, leaving them blocked by bottle necks and red-tape, the lone entrepreneur can move in with not quite legitimate proposals, make profitable arrangements, help every-body, and get things moving, to their and his advan-tage. For example, lawyers, management consultants,

small businessmen, chefs, taxi drivers, can slip the yoke of the system they work in.

2 Isolates are working where the institution gives little scope for autonomy or exercise of authority. They may be found in large numbers in the industrial scene. Bus conductors, supermarket check-out girls, and others with practically no autonomy on the job can find ways of asserting themselves. Their typical response to a system which denies their dignity is to sabotage it.

3 Hierarchists are implementing a division of labour in an organization with ranked levels, responsibility located at each level. Where there is delegation of the work, resulting in remote and weak control, and a require-ment for specialization, they can make up a pilfering gang. Dockers or airport baggage handlers can make a handsome penny on the side if they organize well and remain loyal to their gang.

4 Egalitarian groups have a strong external boundary and weak ranking between members. Roundsmen and hotel workers are among those who flourish at the edges where, the hierarchy's writ having run out, they have scope to make a shared profit.

This framework of opportunism and evasion of control reveals a systematic picture of occupational crime. When Mars turns to another aspect of modern industrial society, the household, his method needs only to be inverted. Research on occupational crime has given him a practised eye for classifying organizations according to the amount of autonomy allowed to each member, the incentives for banding together, and the resort to ranking on the job. The object of the research on crime was to assess indi-viduals' self-assertion against a structure that is already in place.

Households

Gerald Mars and Valerie Mars have now turned their expertise to household structure. For this research the objective is to assess individuals' efforts to build their own organization. The same practised eye can recognize the implications of spatial and temporal divisions and budgetary constraints, but this time they are not being imposed on the subjects. The household organization is created by its members. This approach runs so counter to the usual assumptions and methods of consumer research that it is impossible not to accuse social scientist researchers of 'cultural innocence'. Usual work on consumption behaviour works within the frame of inquiry generated by acknowledged administrative problems. Do we need more hospitals? Do we need more schools? Or prisons? How much Public Assistance, or Public Medicine, can we afford? For such questions the social categories developed by the Registrar General are the most accurate to be had. The population has demographic features, it is classified by age, by sex, by education, by income, by nationality, religion. There is always argument as to whether it is well classified, and the boundaries of the classifications are regularly adjusted. But just as the categories are culturally innocent, so are the arguments. Cultural innocence characterizes a discourse about local politics, a discourse that takes values as given even while arguing normatively about them; a discourse that seeks to persuade and justify action.

Cultural innocence is a dead hand on free inquiry in the social sciences. If all the information we have about household consumption has been collected for these practical purposes, it is unsuited to the profound questions about the motives and intelligence of the shopper that we started with. In those culturally innocent arguments the shopper is a cypher, no more. But the attack on the dignity of the shopper that is implied by swings theories has to be answered at another level. The question raised is not 'Why do these particular people buy these things now?', which is a question located in some culturally defined site; it is 'Why do people ever buy what they buy?', not now, but always? Interest in their choice has been escalated to a meta-cultural level, beyond any local reference. The answers that we have surveyed (which imply a passive shopper responding to swings of fashion or following the market), have to be taken to a different level. Therefore we need information that has been collected specially with intent to test the hypothesis of cultural competition.

The first task is to get some imaginative grip on the idea that family organizations differ culturally. We are used to thinking (in cultural innocence) that the only significant differences between households depend on that very same set of demographic variables that is collected by the Census: number of members, age of members, dependent children, other dependents, work of the bread winner, single parent or not, income, education, employment. There is an implicit idea that if it were not for these differences, families would all be run the same way. To discount such factors, the Mars's (so far unpublished) research chose households that were as alike as possible for all these characteristics. They only examined households that belonged to the same social class, the householders had the same educational level, same numbers and ages – a husband and wife and two children of school age – living in the same kind of locality, suburban duplex units, with the same level of incomes. The differences that they found in organization could not be attributed to these usual explanations, because all the demographic variables were held constant. With a practised eye they looked for use of space and objects and divisions of time, and for division of labour in the home. They carefully checked points in which common budgetary control would be strong or felt not at all. When they had established their index of cultural bias, they revealed four archetypal ways of organizing, linked to four distinct sets of values, attitudes and cosmology.

Once they had found extreme samples of each type, they studied them in detail. They studied the choice of toiletry, choice of foods and choice of methods of preparing them. Gender recognition (as in the choice of colours, towels, wallpapers, newspapers and weeklies), turned out to be an infallible indicator of cultural allegiance, positive in the case of individualist and hierarchical households, and negative in the case of the egalitarian households as one would expect. Some households made a point of playing up gender difference, organizing chores by the sexual division of labour, and developing gender as a prime distinguisher for other choices, as between drinks, say, or soap, toothpaste, shampoo, hair oil and so on. Other households played down gender distinctions, whether for allocating tasks in the home or for any other distributions whatever. It is a pity that this research is not yet published, for the early drafts hinted that when the method was perfected a quick look in the drinks cupboard would predict the contents of the bathroom cupboard, or vice versa, and if both of these cupboards were read correctly they would support a good guess at the range of friends who came into the house and the occasions for their coming. By the time they had finished their fieldwork the Mars had found the clues about time to be so revealing that they could almost identify the cultural allegiance of the household by the response to the request for an appointment.

Hierarchy against the rest

Obviously this was bound to be path-breaking work. Though the detailed consumption items were local to the time and place of the fieldwork, the principles on which it had been designed were general. Questions about how time is distributed, space, work, gender roles, attitudes to authority and equality, such questions could be framed for any part of the world. The principles on which distinct cultures come into conflict over resources are clear enough to generate new questions.[2] For example, it was outside the brief for the Mars's household study to follow up the pattern of relations and friends who were admitted to a given household's celebrations. But presumably hierarchists would spend a lot more time and trouble with inherited friends, and less with work-related friends. One would predict that the hierarchists could be recognized by the number of their parents' friends' children they still see. Funerals and weddings would make another contrast between the two cultural types: hierarchists should be expected to attend relatively more funerals of old family friends, and individualists more weddings of new friends. The individualist household is much more dependent on workplace as a source of friends. Attitudes to sickness and health would be expected to vary along this division.

The existence of distinctive household cultures in itself demonstrates that the different acts of shopping that furnish the different parts of the house are not haphazard responses to particular needs. Some overall pattern is being used. It is not a static, rigid pattern. Cultural theory argues that it emerges afresh in new kinds of commodities every year, every month, every week, because of the opposition between cultures. The array of consumer goods in a house is the surface symptom of an effort to realize a more or less coherent world-view about how a home should be organized. We also realize that shopping is not an exclusively feminine task. The right expression is that the woman 'does the shopping'. She may go to the shops, but the choices she applies are already made in joint choices about what kind of marriage and what kind of home not to have. As far as vindicating the integrity of the shopper, the research goes a long way, but not far enough. That household shopping is a joint affair makes it all the more important to reach into politics, ethics, religion. Nothing said so far shows a link between the organization of the home in terms of age and gender on the one hand, and on the other in terms of attitudes to pesticides, capital punishment, political parties and ideas about the dangers of modern technology.

The question is, do hierarchical rankings between sexes and generations apply beyond the range of the home? Is it unreasonable to expect that the hierarchical family is readier than the individualist family to accept inequality in the larger arena? Does cultural theory predict some homogeneity between the way the domestic scene is constructed and the construction of the rest of the universe? We who are working on cultural theory are divided on this issue. What follows is my own extreme position, which I doubt if anyone else shares completely. I put it as forcibly as I can, with a simple comparison between hierarchy and individualism.

In the hierarchical home there is a strict division of labour: the man does work labelled 'heavy', such as carpentry, work labelled 'emergency', such as unblocking the drains, and work labelled 'technical', such as mending the fuse. He is content that his wife should do regular chores, that are not labelled heavy, emergency or technical, so she cooks and washes the dishes, cleans the house and makes the beds, and of course, she shops. This is the traditional division of labour. It seems reasonable that this background should predispose him to divisions of labour in general. He can be expected to combine with his wife in setting up what Bernstein (1971) has called 'the positional family' a structure of relations in which everyone has an allotted place. His children are dealt with according to gender and age. The chores they are allotted follow the same principles as followed for the parents. Their bed times reflect the age differentials: eldest has privileges in virtue of being first born. Thus there is a rooted expectation of inequality between the sexes and between ages. To me it seems obvious that this would be carried forward from the confines of the home to the rest of their life. Is it not this same man who makes 'Yorkshire jokes' in the pub with his mates? Yorkshire jokes are affectionate stories about how odd of women to want to go out to work, and how the wife's work costs more than she earns, and how funny women are about shopping. With good luck, the wife in this home has her circle of cronies with whom she makes the equivalent jokes about how funny men are.

For contrast, take the individualist at home: this husband does the shopping and shares the washing up; he is not going to be able to laugh in the pub with the ones who don't. But then, he is not very likely to be drinking with them anyway and he can laugh at Yorkshire jokes somewhere else. Industrial society has its own division of labour: some occupations provide an all-male workplace, which would be congruent with the sexual division of labour in the home. At this point we need to face our own preferences.

Hierarchy, individualism and enclave egalitarianism are incompatible organizing principles. We are each bound to prefer one type of culture to the others. It is inevitable and right to have a preference. But cultural innocence should not obscure our professional judgement. One type of culture is not ineluctably, eternally better than another. There is currently a general prejudice in favour of the egalitarian home, in favour of the individualist home, or of attempted compromise combinations of the two, and a strong prejudice among social science professionals against the hierarchical home. Is this antipathy for hierarchy culturally innocent? The division of labour generally gives expectations of more prestige and higher lifetime income to those employed in the service industries than to those in manufacturing and extraction industries. It is in the latter that sexual segregation is strongest and where we are most likely to find the hierarchical domestic culture. It is possible that the current rejection of the hierarchical home is partly simple snobbism, partly opportunism, a conforming preference for an elite lifestyle. The child brought up in the individualist regime has a chance of profiting well from the opportunities of contemporary life. But there are costs. The hierarchical culture is destructive in some ways, the individualist culture is destructive in others. The hierarchical household is less likely than the individualist household to fall apart when calamity strikes. If the wife is struck with a crippling disease, if a child is severely handicapped, if the husband becomes permanently unemployed, the hierarchical home has more resources for dealing with the tragedy. For one thing, at least if either of the parents is incapacitated, it is an advantage to have friends who are not based on the workplace.

New research

A complex and subtle interlacing connects the domestic cultural bias with that of the occupational structure.

Though religious affiliation might be the same, or education, or income level, the Mars's research suggests that
the jokes will not be the same. And the politics will not be
the same. We would expect that caring for the environment, caring for equality and worrying about risks of
technology would all go together. Respect for the established professions, suspicion of alternative medicine,
worrying about the influx of foreigners would be another
bundle of concerns. It is not daring to predict a connection,
but in fact it has not been revealed by the surveys of
lifestyles and values. The empirical data to support this
argument have been hard to assemble. The reason is that
domestic cultural bias has been ignored.

So consumer studies are left with the surprising
possibility that a man has one attitude to his wife in the
home and another attitude to women in general. It is still
possible to believe, against intuition, that no connections
hold regularly between home life and life at work. Since
the idea of the hierarchical home has not been the object of
study, we cannot tell whether it generates a desire for a
new social order with greater concern for the environment
– I would expect not. Does domestic hierarchy support
egalitarian politics? I would say, No, impossible, or most
unlikely. Does domestic hierarchy go with green politics?
Does domestic individualism support green politics? I
would expect not. We will never know, so long as the
market researchers are convinced that the significant
differences between homes are registered in the Census. If
the market researchers believe that cultural bias in national
politics is independent of domestic politics, crucial
information about the noble art of shopping will never
be collected and we will all be left with our prejudices.

Fortunately for the strong version of cultural theory,
research to test it is now being developed. Given their

professional training, it is natural that psychologists should look for individual personality differences to explain attitudes to dangers from technology. The change of direction comes from work on perception of risk. It was difficult to get acceptance for the first work on this subject (Douglas and Wildavsky, 1982). The breakthrough started with a survey that asked respondents about their attitudes to risks from specific technologies and at the same time sought to link their answers with one of two world-views (Buss et al., 1985). Contemporary World-View A offers a high-growth, high-technology, free-enterprise society, with a pro-business stance on goals and governance. Contemporary World-View B offers a future in which material and technical growth will level off, and in which governments will be concerned for social and environmental welfare, redistribution of wealth from richer to poorer nations, participative decision-making and non-materialistic values. In terms of cultural theory, the survey asked about political preferences between two cultural types; World-View A is individualist, World-View B is egalitarian enclavist. The result of the survey showed strong correlations between political world-view and perceptions of danger from technology. Since then more empirical results have connected attitudes to risk with cultural bias (Dake and Wildavsky, 1990).

We are on the track of the connection between the choice among pesticides and the differential bed-times of children, if there is one. We will soon know whether the preference for artificial fertilizers versus organic gardening is linked to Yorkshire jokes and the rules for washing the dishes. When the results of new surveys which are now being designed have appeared, we will discover whether the principles that run the home normally stay within the home. My predilection is for expecting the connection to be very close. If the new data now being collected by Michael Thompson, Karl Dake and Aaron Wildavsky[3] support the strong hypothesis, then we are on the way to a comprehensive cultural theory that will connect preferences among commodities to preferred lifestyles, and these to the economic structure of the society.

Though this programme sounds familiar enough to make sense we have not been able to exploit it theoretically because empirical support was lacking. The assumption that shopping is an expression of individual wants misdirected all our inquiries. Consumer research had succeeded in turning round the normal everyday expectation. Most people generally assume that these cultural and occupational connections are there, and that shopping is a fully rational activity, but consumer theory introduced utterly implausible limitations on that rationality. All we have to do now is to go back to common sense and take account of cultural bias. The idea of consumer sovereignty in economic theory will be honoured in market research, because it will be abundantly clear that the shopper sets the trends, new technology and new prices are adjuncts to achieving the shopper's goal. The shopper is not expecting to develop a personal identity by choice of commodities: that would be too difficult. Shopping is an agonistic struggle to define not what one is, but what one is not. When we include not one cultural bias, but four, and when we allow that each is bringing its critique against the others, and when we see that the shopper is adopting postures of cultural defiance, then it all makes sense.

Notes

1 Miller (1991) gives a summary of the writings in this vein.

On not being seen dead

2 Michael Thompson and Karl Dake are developing Gerald Mars's pilot study for a large-scale test, but this is not ready to publish.
3 Aaron Wildavsky died in 1993.

References

Bernstein, B. (1971) *Class, Codes and Control*, vol. 1, *Theoretical Studies Towards a Sociology of Language*. London: Routledge & Kegan Paul.

Buss, D.M., Craik, K.H. and Dake, K.M. (1985) 'Perception of decision procedures for managing and regulating hazards', in F. Homberger (ed.), *Safety Evaluation and Regulation*. New York: Karger. pp. 199–208.

Dake, K. and Wildavsky, A. (1990) 'Theories of risk perception: who fears what and why?', *Deadalus, Risk*, 119(4): 41–60.

Douglas, M. and Wildavsky, A. (1982) *Risk and Culture: an Essay on the Selection of Technical and Environmental Dangers*. Berkeley, CA: University of California Press.

Goodman, N. (1978) *Ways of Worldmaking*. Indianapolis: Hackett.

Mars, G. (1982) *Cheats at Work: an Anthropology of Workplace Crime*. London: Allen & Unwin.

Mars, G. and Mars, V. (no date) *The Creation of Household Cultures* (originally commissioned as a report for Unilever, now being developed with new empirical enquiries).

Miller, D. (1991) 'Appropriating the state on the council estate', *Man*, 23: 352–72.

Schwarz, M. and Thompson, M. (1990) *Divided We Stand: Redefining Politics, Technology and Social Choice*. Brighton: Harvester-Wheatsheaf.

Thompson, M. (1988) 'Socially viable ideas of nature', in E. Baark and U. Svedin (eds), *Nature, Culture, Technology: Towards a New Conceptual Framework*. London: Macmillan.

Thompson, M., Ellis, R. and Wildavsky, A. (1990) *Cultural Theory*. Boulder, CO: Westview Press.

Thompson, M., Warburton, M. and Hately, T. (1986) *Uncertainty on a Himalayan Scale: an Institutional Theory of Environmental Perception and a Strategic Framework for a Sustainable Development of the Himalaya*. London: Milton Ash Editions Ethnographica.

5

The Consumer's Revolt

Mindless consumerism

Some consumers accuse others of mindlessness, of practising mindless consumerism, or worse than mindless, of morally wrong consumerism. In this chapter I am not exactly defending consumerism, but I am putting the question of conscience in context with the idea of consumer rationality. The argument will be that most consciences tend to fall into a muddle, and that the consumerist is not more muddled morally than other consumers. What we should be objecting to, if we object to mindless consumerism, is something about the culture and social organization to which it belongs. But when we face the issue, we find that we are in something of a dilemma, if not a muddle, about our own consumer choices.

I start with a story about non-consuming, actually about non-consuming of headgear. One day when I was in my early twenties, I met my Great-Aunt Ethel in Regent Street. To me it was a lovely surprise as she lived in Dorset, but she seemed less than delighted to see me. As soon as our greetings were done, she spoke her worry: 'Don't tell your grandmother that you saw me in London without a hat.' Since childhood she had rebelled against her eldest sister's judgement, and her adult choices continued to express nervous revolt against my grandmother. Her great-nieces admired her zest and originality. An army widow on a small pension, she none the less led a splendidly independent life; a caravan-dweller, a painter, the bohemian artist in the family, she was way ahead of the others in modernity. She raised angora rabbits and ran a troop of Wolf Cubs. She ate nuts and fruit, and wore bright handwoven garments, wooden beads, brilliant embroidered waistcoats which set off her white hair. Much later we realized that she was not a lone rebel when we recognized the influence of the Arts and Crafts Movement. Other people were making the same rebellion against bourgeois taste, refusing to be mindless victims of industrial society.

To know why people do consume, we need to understand why they sometimes do not. Where do they get the strength of mind to resist? When the stuff is there, when credit is available, when the shops flaunt their wares, when the advertisements wave it under their noses, how do they manage to resist? It is the other side of the puzzle about why sometimes people pass up a chance to earn more: the wages are good, they have the time, transport is no problem, but they just do not come forward to be enrolled in the labour market. Preference for leisure and resistance to the appeal of goods are two sides of the same coin and what explains one should explain the other. Mindless consumption means being drawn willy-nilly into the snares of the capitalist market system. Paradoxically, refusing to choose higher wages is also dubbed irrational, a mindless refusal to better oneself.

Of course, there was nothing mindless about Great-Aunt Ethel's consumption pattern: it was austere, and economical; the message was well targeted. She was in favour of freedom and modern principles of hygiene, against stuffy custom for custom's sake, and against the machine age. She would have been against 'consumerism' if the

107

word had been around. It is alleged that what is wrong with the consumer society is that consumption goods have become commodities, desired for their own sake, used for personal advantage, comfort or display. Mindless consumerism is part of a trend that has made our culture victim to commoditization, and exposed us to predatory advertisers and media. It is assumed therefore to be part of a relatively modern problem, the disembedding of thought and behaviour from preindustrial matrices.

My interest today is in whether we have to consent to reducing our whole personhood to a passive role in maintaining the capitalist system. I wish someone would tell me what to do about it. Are we helpless inhabitants of capitalist industrial society? If consumerism is bad, do we have no responsibility as consumers? Keeping a check on the producers is a good thing to do, and obviously necessary, but it can only be part of the answer. If we are really not passively programmed, are there no steps we can take to correct our own purchasing habits? Should we withdraw, grow our own food? (Much more expensive of course.) Should we buy clothes woven by cottage industries? (Also very expensive, and inclined to be baggy.) Restrict our travel? When a recent Indian prime minister, mindful of Gandhi's example, declared that he would only use public transport, the problems of his security guards became overwhelming. The same for the mayor of New York who started out by refusing to live in the mayoral mansion, believing his own humble abode in Greenwich Village gave better signals about his politics. If enough of us withdrew from the industrial system, it would throw thousands more out of work. Thoreau's account of his exemplary retreat to Walden reads chillingly false, because he could come out of it any time he wanted, more like Marie Antoinette playing at being a dairy maid than a model of social protest. There must be some other way than opting out.

First we should question the association of the consumer society with capitalist production. The grand sweep of modern history makes it inevitable that we should associate the two. The search for luxuries by new rich, the politics of class competition, the pressure to marry up, the uses of goods to perfect seduction, the political aspects are all there together. In an excellent survey of the historical evidence, Arjun Appadurai cuts through the difficulties of defining luxury goods. They are for him:

> goods whose principal use is rhetorical and social, goods that are simply incarnated signs. The necessity to which they respond is fundamentally political. Better still, since most luxury goods are used (though in special ways and at special cost), it might make more sense to regard luxury as a special 'register' of consumption (by analogy to the linguistic model), than to regard them as a special class of things. (1986, p. 38)

He must be right there, but I suspect he is mistaken in restricting the idea of luxury to the choices of privileged elites. The signs of being in the register of luxuries he takes to be the following: restriction to elites, complexity of acquisition, a 'semiotic virtuosity' of being capable of signalling complex messages, specialized knowledge for right consumption, and closely linked to body, person and personality.

This definition works if one is mainly already interested in the historical process of our own society. However, since something very like consumerism rears its head in different parts of the world, at different times, it may be useful to take a narrower sweep (Hamilton and Lai, 1989). Restriction to elites in this narrower view is not an essential element in the idea of a luxury. Any community or family, completely egalitarian, may use a sign that some days, or some persons, or occasions need to be celebrated with specially rare consumption. The delightful idea of 'semiotic virtuosity' is a characteristic that may be endowed on any thing at all, and so no help in defining luxury. From the five criteria suggested, we are left then with three signs of luxury: complexity of acquisition, specialized knowledge in consumption, and serving directly the body and person. In short, luxuries are for the purpose of special marking of events and persons. Once selected to do that marking, they acquire 'semiotic virtuosity'. When what had been accounted as luxuries become widely and indiscriminately used, we generally find that something else has happened: the local community controls have weakened. Consumerism cannot take hold unless enough individuals have been liberated from sumptuary laws and local standardized patterns of consumption. Their release from control generates a real demand for goods that minister to personal comfort, well-being and display. A strong flow of income and goods floods past the filtering screen that has been checking the gates of demand. Individuals suddenly find themselves able to defy custom, to buy what they want to buy, wear seductive clothes and jewellery, eat exotic foods. Should we grudge them their rebellion?

Consumerism starts as a liberation. If nothing else, the liberation is from drudgery. In Raymond Williams's great novel about a Welsh village in the 1920s, *Border Country* (1960/1964), there are several conversations about the relative merits of consumer comforts versus the old way. For example, this description of a new bungalow:

> no old stone floors, no muck in the yard, no miles to go to the shops. We got the electric, see, and the gas for cooking, and the car and the good water, and the you know, the proper W.C. I often say to Janie I was born in Glynmawr but I

wouldn't go back there to live for anybody. Not if they paid me. Don't I, Janie? . . . Out there, in Glynmawr you know, talking. Why, I ask them, do we put up with dirty old water, and oil lamps, and the buckets, you know the buckets? (1960/ 1964, pp. 153–4)

This theme of personal comfort and freedom compared with living at close quarters and under each other's watchful eye runs through the book. Formerly they used to be content to live four or five to a room, now they all want a house for their own family; in the end the valley is going to be destroyed by the people moving out. No one could wish them to stay with the drudgery. It is the same for us and our liking for better kitchens and lighting, easier housework, more freedom to meet each other in distant places. As we extend the lines of our consumption rituals, we too demolish our local communities. The problem is still with us.

But the consumers' revolt is not just against the drudgery. It is a revolt against the despotism of neighbours whose business it is to know and judge everything that is done, what food is eaten, what time the children are put to bed, who is seducing whom and who is wearing clothes that look too seductive by local standards. A consumerist is one who defends the right of a person to be free from a neighbour's tyranny over his or her consumption habits. I insist on consumerism as a form of revolt, not just to be fair to the consumerists, but to put modern consumerism into context. Anyone who feels passionately that consumerism is wrong should be consistent. Are they ready to defend the constraints which hold consumerism in check? The goods that people can buy respond to some extent to the demands that these same people make on each other and these respond to the kind of society.

The basic choice is not between kinds of goods, but between kinds of society, and, for the interim, between the kinds of position in society that are available to us as we line up in the debate about transforming society. When we have made up our mind where we want to be aligned, do we have much free choice about the judgements we are going to make about goods? According to Pierre Bourdieu (1979), no, our preference for kinds of food and drink, housing and clothing is part of the bundle that we initially choose as we align ourselves in the political debate, and even for that alignment, he would say that we do not have much choice.

The scheme works remarkably well for French society because of the social stability provided by the Grandes Ecoles and the control that they ensure for the establishment. It gives a rational explanation of choices among goods: preferences are enrolled in the contest for supremacy. In so far as the French workers are not interested in aesthetic judgements that will never give them access to power, they are off the map. That in itself is a weakness in the theory. Another weakness is that it does not explain how goods are chosen in a community in which everyone is more or less equally well endowed. That is to say, it leaves out of account the kinds of consumption patterns found in many of the egalitarian societies anthropologists study. The scheme is good for making us aware of how politicized our taste is, and so good for attacking the economists' theory of the consumer as an individual sovereignly exercising private preferences. It does explain stable pockets of resistance to the wiles of the media, but it does *not* explain apparently mindless succumbing to the media's suggestions. It is consumer mindlessness that disturbs all the theories and creates the basic reproach to the capitalist system.

The constitutional monitor

To show consumerism as a kind of cultural revolt we need to take a step back from the northern European scene. Cultural theory is expected to apply to Africa, the Mediterranean, anywhere. It starts with the individual making his or her choices about what company to keep. Other people are the prime problem and on this theory every item of the human and material environment is drawn upon as a resource for dealing with other people. This starting point differs from market research which assumes that each individual is encircled by personal needs of greater or less urgency, physical needs first, then social, then spiritual satisfactions. It is a kind of mad nightmare, as if the average shopper were hungry, naked and roofless, and needs first to assure his next meal, then looks to his clothes from the point of view of warmth and protection from the cold and rain, then he is ready to see to his family and their physical needs, and only when all this is done, turns to the rest of the world in a more benignly philanthropic mood.

Instead of starting from the individual confronting his own basic needs, cultural theory starts from a stable system in which a consumer knows that he is expected to play some part or he will not get any income. In this theory the consumer has what can be called a cultural project. Everything that he chooses to do or to buy is part of a project to choose other people to be with who will help him to make the kind of society he thinks he will like the best. It is as if there were inside his head a little monitor for the constitutional effects that would flow from generalizing the present state of affairs. If he wants not to be dominated, he steers clear of some kinds of persons whose domineering habits he can instantly recognize. If he

113

wants stability, he steers clear of revolutionary others who seem to be inveterate upsetters of apple carts. Steering clear of some, he steers towards others, reading their signals and emitting his own. The signals are, of course, the so-called consumption goods. The constitutional monitor is the elementary background of consumption patterns and consumer behaviour, and even of consumerism.

Another way of presenting this might be to say that the consumer is always engaged in making a collective good. The forms of consumption which he prefers are those that maintain the kind of collectivity he likes to be in. The theory takes account of four kinds of cultural preference.[1]

1 One would be the ideal liberal preference for a society which allows the members uninhibited opportunity to negotiate and transact: the collective good would be a minimum of fair play rules such as ensure the working of a free market.
2 Another would be a preference for the society in which a chap has the right to be left alone, without any wish to negotiate for power or authority. It would be a community of isolates, or drop-outs, or hermits.
3 The third is a preference for collaboration in a rationally integrated society.[2] This pattern restricts opportunism for the sake of protecting the categories and compartments it is prepared to defend.
4 The above can be very restrictive social environments. Rather than be subordinated in the first type by fellow members more competitive than he, or in the second type rather than put up with the poverty and neglect that are generally the lot of drop-outs, and rather than accept the control of a strongly ordered system such as hierarchy, another cultural choice would be to band together with a few like-minded souls to make a

protected enclave, protesting against those who want to domineer.

The first two leave the shopper exposed and vulnerable. The last two choices are for forms of corporate grouping, one structured, one unstructured. Both of them have inherent powers of resistance to the temptations of consumerism. In what follows I shall argue that anyone who seriously disapproves of consumerism must logically be bound to support the choice for a communitarian way of life. That would be an uncomfortable choice for many of the most articulate anticonsumerists.

Cream buns and private transport

The thesis is that a community controls mindless spending like a person controls mindless consuming of cigarettes or cream buns . . . by making alternative desires effective. The parallel between the person's and the community's objectives has been proposed by Tom Schelling (1978) and worked out by Jon Elster (1985) in an essay that conflates the prisoner's dilemma problem of a community with that of the person who entertains conflicting goals one of which, if reached, will make the others impossible. An example of 'weakness of will', or *akrasia*, is the individual person who wants a svelte, athletic figure but who cannot resist a high calorie diet. One of his objectives lies further in the future than the other; the cream bun is here and the desire for it is now, the pleasing answer on the weighing machine or in the mirror is in the future, and is postponed. Or the desired cream bun seems a minor interruption of the main plan to reduce weight; it is conceded because it is so inconsequential to the success of the main project. In the same way, free-riders on the collective effort persuade themselves that now is more important than a remote

115

future, or that one little private bonus siphoned off from the community fund for a private purpose will be too inconsequential to matter. So though all Londoners deplore the havoc created by unlimited private transport, those who have cars will use them rather than the buses and underground and there is weakness of will as to how to solve the resultant traffic problem. Likewise, for another London example, most Londoners are ready to deplore the destruction of the small corner shops by competition from the supermarkets. But they show weakness of will whenever they take their car down to the supermarket car park and stock up for the month. Their own contribution to the commons despoiled is too inconsequential to count, and economic rationality seems to win the day, for the corner shop is much more expensive: why should my family be taxed to keep them in business?

On this view consumerism is no more difficult to explain than the failure to control impulse eating or smoking. The curious thing would be that control was ever successfully exerted and sustained. I will argue that if there is going to be a community at all it will impose disciplines, to use Foucault's expression, on the body and on the mind. The disciplines will be painful, and therefore will instigate revolt. If the revolt is successful there are two likely outcomes. One is the revolt of the disciplined, calculated withdrawal, such as refusing to wear hats, an amazingly difficult thing to do in isolation, a sign of great strength of will. The other is to reject both the discipline and the community that exerts the control.

Community despotism

In spite of a large literary documentation of its tyranny, the sentimental idea of community prevails. I have already

116

protested against the distortion this has produced in the theory of consumption (Douglas, 1980, 1986), but it may still be worth making more stark the case that community is repressive and costs a lot. To start with, go the Musée des Arts Traditionnels et Populaires in Paris, and admire the presentation of a Breton homestead; note the small scale, the paucity of utensils, the economy of storage space, the high degree of order needful for four or five persons to live in the confined quarters; above all, note the standardization of costume, artefacts and decoration. On another wall, arrays of knives, hooks, lace testify to strong local definition. Why is everything so standardized that an amateur can quickly recognize a regional product?

The community, any community, exists because it constitutes a separate claim on the purses and time and energy of its members. There is no community unless its members concede its right to fund itself by levies upon themselves. For their part, the dues they pay are an investment, and they exact corresponding rights. This is a transactional approach to consumption, it requires that the community is one of the agents transacting, or at least that other agents transact on its behalf. The approach requires a distinction between a house and a home, or between a village and a community. 'What a lovely home you have!' exclaimed an American visitor on entering a house for the first time. In England it would be a nonsense sentence, since the house may be lovely without there being any home in it at all. The same for some Cotswold villages where netted thatch and manicured gardens are no guarantee of any community at all.

In *Border Country*, the novel quoted above, the young wife likes to go shopping, but she does not spend on herself: she buys things 'for the house' (Williams, 1960/1964, p. 57) Curtains, cushions, china represent a levy on the

householder's purse for the commons. It is taken for granted
that the house has a claim on the family budget, a kind of tax
on members for their common life together. In the same way
a village community has a claim on the purses and energies
of its members. It imposes its informal taxes. No one can live
in the community and escape paying out for condolences,
christenings, name day celebrations, the police force dance,
the life-boat fund. Some of the dues make a circulating fund,
like the Cargas of the Latin American fiestas. Some are
centrally collected and disbursed.[3] A Breton colleague told
me of how, as a boy at his grandmother's funeral, he was
posted at the door of the church to make a list of all the
families which had given the priest a contribution for a Mass
to be said for her soul: it was *de rigueur* for his family to
reciprocate in kind on the death of any member of
the families listed. Though the reciprocity went between
families, the donations went to the church and would be
eventually disbursed among its other charitable *oeuvres*.
Paying is not enough: there has also to be a physical
presence. In an English farming community everyone has to
go to the Hunt Ball, as well as contribute to it. Turning up at
the event is one of the ways by which the community knows
who its members are, a kind of informal census-taking.
Furthermore, when a big crowd turns out, to see the May
dances, or the Saint's Day fireworks or the cricket match,
community solidarity is made visible. More significantly, the
requirement to be present and to pay the equivalent of a
community tax channels the earnings of members towards
the community itself. The heavier the communal chores and
dues, the stronger the sign of commitment.

Some communities recognize that gross disparity in
incomes will be disruptive, and so they use the levies for
public events for redistributive purposes. Individual sur-
pluses are drawn out of private hands and neutralized or

destroyed. In parts of Africa when an important person dies, masses of valuables are buried with him, with the result that debts are cancelled, accumulations run down. The same intention to reduce excessive accumulation may lie behind the Iron Age burials, and certainly they would have had that effect. For example, some Mediterranean villagers display finery in their churches that contrasts with the poverty of their homes: public affluence along with private squalor, to turn Kenneth Galbraith's phrase around. The money that has gone to pay for chandeliers or marble pillars might well have reduced the labour of buckets and scrubbing dirty old stone floors in the kitchens. What Max Weber mistakenly saw as other-worldliness in medieval Christianity was usually a sign of strong this-worldliness, a consumption decision in favour of the community at the expense of the individual.

At the same time, the public demand that absorbs private wealth is the consumers' parallel to the workforce that condemns rate busting. Marshall Sahlins has suggested that many hunting and gathering tribes in Australia and Africa should be called the first affluent societies, because of their high preference for leisure and the shortness of their working day (Sahlins, 1972). In many cases, they are not preferring leisure to the rewards of work, but acceding to the demands of the community that they be present for mourning, rejoicing, eating, praying or dancing together. They have adjusted to a low level of private wants partly because of the high taxes that their community exacts.[4]

I will now speak about the community for convenience as if it were a person with intentions and ideas. The community recognizes that the money earned cannot be stretched to all possible desires. Orlove and Rutz point out that certain expenditures indicate present and future intentions to withdraw: in Indonesia, poor peasants will take the wearing of imported cloth by cosmopolitans to suggest a partial withdrawal from sponsorship of ceremonies . . . The motor-cycles are in some sense an investment, in that money spent on a motor-cycle reduces the expenditures on transport and allows easier access to outside markets; they might well also be a source of individual pleasure, and they indicate to others an orientation beyond the village. They commit the owners to the future acquisition of monetary income beyond subsistence needs, for purchase of gasoline and spare parts . . . (1989, pp. 8–9)

Two worries concern the stakeholders who want the community to survive. One is that members may go away. They do go, and emigrants who return to their village are mercilessly milked by the relatives who have stayed behind. They should not have gone; people have died, and they were not there; now that they have come back, they have to be generous. No wonder the migrant worker tries to make huge savings before he can face his family. The other worry is shouldering liability for its old, infirm and indigent. The community applauds those who look after their old. In a way, earning that applause is like a pension fund. Those who have invested in the community all their lives expect to be cared for by someone or other near to them, and they all watch keenly for defectors. The community will be hard on anyone on whom the old or helpless have an unfulfilled claim, and everyone will be engaged in rebutting claims. This one was always drunk, no wonder he has no savings, that one played the horses, it is his own fault if he is stranded now, the other one was quarrelsome, too proud, irreligious. The community finds itself applying standards of good husbandry, health and hygiene, as excuses. If anyone falls into debt through their own fault, the community is not going to be so generous with credit. The acceptance of liability justifies the sumptuary controls, the criticism of extravagance, drinking and gambling. The community withdraws its protection from the deviants. It has to be assured that its members not only pay their dues now, but are likely to be able to continue to do so. Hence a pressure against spending, a time preference for the future, and a general tyranny over private consumption.

Anyone who has invested in such a community has expectations from it. Paying his dues, he does not expect other men to seduce his wife or daughters. Paying his dues, he does not expect other men's wives or daughters to seduce him, or his sons, or otherwise to upset his plans for marriage alliances. Hence some of the disciplines of the body, and the standardization of clothing, decoration and everything to do with sex. To belong to such a community means accepting its standards. Eccentricity is rejected, flamboyancy reproved as much as carelessness. Hence the standardization of objects. Excellence of artisanship has to be achieved without conspicuousness. Economy, wit, proportion, scale, accommodation to function and storage, these are the limits on craft work for the everyday utensils that we so much admire. Artistic display, originality, extravagance may be deployed for objects of public ownership. Everyday objects are minutely graded to their uses. Special objects are endowed with semiotic richness and their consumption is hedged with rules, so that they can mark the occasions when the community celebrates itself. The objects are coded, and to know the coding is a claim to membership. This is the basis of the tyranny which embeds every consumption choice in a communication system. Here there is no problem of how a person finds the strength to resist the lures of commodities; the strength is in the surveillance of neighbours, backed by the security of the local community. Anyone who has been a member of such a community knows that it takes more courage to move out than to remain embedded.

Rational consumption

Though this picture draws upon a rather commonplace knowledge of consumption patterns, it has merit in setting up the community chest and the private purse agonistically as rivals. It explains why the community scrutinizes its members' consumption so critically, and judges so harshly any deviation. The more fragile the community bond, the more anxious and severe the scrutiny and the more fuel to the fires of revolt. There is nothing irrational about deciding to invest socially (Orlove and Rutz's expression) or in deciding to invest and spend on a personal basis. Consumerist, or anticonsumerist, both choices are reasonable. However, symmetry is lacking. It is always feasible to have a programme of consumption for oneself. A programme of community investment may be unreasonable, since it depends on ongoing support from other people.

Returning to the four cultural projects which we sketched at the beginning, each of them presents the rational person with a goal, the kind of society he would like to live in. Given the goal, it is rational that consumption should be engaged to serve it, and that conscience should be invoked to uphold the pattern. In the case of the liberal preference for a society upheld by rules of free play, the person's buying pattern may reflect a conscious revolt against community despotism. In the case of the drop-out, who wants a society where he can be left in peace, the prior dignity of a life of contemplation may justify his erratic but low expenditure. In the enclave the conscience of members has been stirred in protest against the liberal pursuit of personal ease and comfort. In the rationally integrated community the conscience is towards collective survival, so that incipient defectors are admonished. So where is there any irrationality?

Most consumer revolts are symbolic, gestures of independence, like Great-Aunt Ethel's rejection of hats. However, moving out of the range of the community's censorship, there are traps to ensnare the deserter. Choosing to be free of the community censure involves choosing to be a society where each finds his allies by his own efforts, a competitive society in which consumption is inevitably competitive. This is the field well described by Thorstein Veblen and many others. But it would be a great mistake to suppose that competitive consumption is mindless. In a competitive world signals of success attract allies and business; consumption can easily be harnessed to making those signals. Then it is that luxuries and necessities become confused, and total disembedding gives an air of disordered consumerism. Only relatively stable communities can make and keep a distinction between luxuries and necessities. What other people call luxuries appear higgledy-piggledy on the consumerist's plate or in his bedroom and bathroom. The truth is that consumerism is part of a highly competitive way of living, in which everything may be dragged in to the purpose of pleasing a client or ally. Competitive consumerism needs luxuries all the time for a rational deployment of resources. Competition needs to tear down community boundaries, to expand the range of its dealings. There is no surprise that it scoffs at the restraints on spending as well as the disciplines of the body which keep consumption within bounds.

Consumerism is not in itself irrational; what would be irrational would be for the very persons to voice a worry about the environment who demand private transport in the metropolis. The very ones who worry about the absence of community solidarity should not drive the small urban corner shops out of business by shopping in the supermarkets. Rational behaviour puts its money where its mouth is and recognizes community levies and taxes for what they are.

Notes

1 Cultural theory focuses on four possible kinds of social environment, argues that these are the stable, viable kinds of society and that others are on a transitional course between one or other of them; also that in any community there are pressures to transform the present constitution into one or another type, and that these pressures are manifest in a regular normative debate. Furthermore, each kind of culture defines itself by contrast to and against the attraction of others. There is an extensive literature developing the theory and illustrating and challenging it. For a bibliography, see Thompson et al. (1990).

2 The same four cultural types can be defined according to the type of integration, and the amount of integration preferred: the liberal ideal will produce integration based on economic efficiency, and on the power that accumulates where wealth is held; the isolates prefer as little integration as possible, hoping thus to be left alone; the enclavists because they are integrated on a principle of voluntary protest, are organized with reference to their outer boundary; those who prefer an integration that will organize a wide sweep of positive communitarian goals, are trying to build a collectivity which will in practice focus on several mutually balancing institutional centres.

3 Compare Karl Polyani's analysis of gift exchange patterns in ancient civilizations which he explicitly compared with household distribution. Here I am turning the analogy the other way round.

4 For an interesting discussion of these debates, see Ahrne (1988).

References

Ahrne, G. (1988) 'A labour theory of consumption', in Per Otnes (ed.), *The Sociology of Consumption*. Oslo: Solum Forlag. pp. 50–2.

Appadurai, Arjun (1986) *The Social Life of Things: Commodities in Cultural Perspective*. Cambridge: Cambridge University Press.

Bourdieu, P. (1979) *La Distinction*. Paris: Editions Minuit.

Douglas, M. (1980) *The World of Goods*. New York: Basic Books.

Douglas, M. (1986) *How Institutions Think*. New York: Syracuse University Press. ch. 3.

Elster, J. (1985) 'Weakness of will and the free-rider problem', *Economics and Philosophy*, 1: 231–65.

Hamilton, G.G. and Lai, Chi-kong (1989) 'Consumerism without capitalism: consumption and brand names in late Imperial China', in B. Orlove and H.J. Rutz (eds), *The Social Economy of Consumption: Monographs in Economic Anthropology, No. 6*. Washington, DC: University Press of America. pp. 253–80.

Orlove, B. and Rutz, H.J. (1989) 'Thinking about consumption', in *The Social Economy of Consumption: Monographs in Economic Anthropology, No. 6*. Washington, DC: University Press of America.

Sahlins, Marshall (1972) *Stone Age Economics*. Chicago: Aldine-Atherton.

Schelling, T. (1978) 'Egonomics, or the art of self-management', *American Economic Review: Papers and Proceedings*, 68: 290–4.

Thompson, M., Wildavsky, A. and Ellis, R. (1990) *Cultural Theory*. Boulder, CO: Westview Press.

Williams, R. (1960/1964) *Border Country*. London: Chatto & Windus. Quotations from Penguin edn, 1964.

6

Anomalous Animals and Animal Metaphors

Here follows a warning against two common ideas about symbolism. One is against the unwary use of anomaly. The other is the same warning against metaphor. When I have explained the traps I will suggest a way of avoiding them.

The idea that perception of an anomalous animal kind comes to us out of the nature of biological orders can be firmly laid aside. Animal anomalies are not installed in nature but emerge from particular features of classificatory schemes. In *Purity and Danger* (1966) I thought that this was to say enough. I focused on the 'nonfit'. Since no scheme of classification can cover the infinite variety of experience there will always be elements that do not fit. Then it is a matter of cultural idiosyncrasy as to which elements escape through the meshes of the classifications, and of cultural bias as to whether they are noticed at all, and whether, if they are noticed as anomalous, this provokes any special interest, either of approval or distaste. The programme that then seemed to lie ahead was to examine the social conditions that demand very concise and exhaustive classifications and those that encourage a lax attitude to fit and misfit. Questions about classification, rather than questions about the identification of particular anomalies or metaphors, have been the centre of my interests, starting with *Natural Symbols* (1970) and going on to the present. The programme does not help to interpret metaphors or to recognize anomalies since it focuses only on features of classification that are sustained by practical use, so at first sight it is not easy for me to have something to say about animal symbolism. But there are many things that have to be said about interpretations of metaphors and anomalies in general that could perhaps be helpful.

It is obviously wrong to say that a thing is anomalous by using our own categories. It is not even enough to argue from our idea of nature to natural anomalies, such as flightless birds, flying fish, or barkless dogs. We should not expect that what we regard as deviant sub-species widely distributed across oceans and deserts would be accorded special taxonomic status in all cultures. Bulmer (1986) tested this in trying to trace the prohibited birds in Leviticus 11 and Deuteronomy 13, but was forced to conclude that the evidence did not stand up.

An anthropologist who claims to know that a particular animal or human kind is perceived as an anomaly in the foreign culture needs to justify the claim. But how? The right way for the anthropologist to deal with suspected anomalies will be the same right way to deal with metaphors. Most of the analyses of the symbolism of animals show the animal kingdom as a projection or metaphor of social life; the analysis depends implicitly on resemblance or picturing. It may be directly, as when the animal is said to depict particular human feelings, such as compassion or cruelty. Or more indirectly, as when by their industry or unruliness, for instance, they are taken to represent certain kinds of human behaviour. All metaphorical identifications depend on making a match. The exercise is to identify some sameness in both fields. However, there is no limit to the power of the imagination for seeing patterns and finding resemblances. So there is no limit to the scope for finding similarity between any sets of objects.

Similarity is not a quality of things in themselves, as Goodman (1972) points out. He makes seven strictures against treating similarity as explanation. The first stricture relates to his concern for a better understanding of the nature of abstraction and realism in art:

> Similarity does not distinguish any symbols as peculiarly 'iconic', or account for the grading of pictures as more or less realistic or conventional.
> Representation does not depend on resemblance alone.

Similarity is relative, variable and culture-dependent.

The second stricture is that similarity does not pick out replicas. The third applies the second to events; two performances of the same work may be very different, repetitions of the same behaviour may involve widely varying sequences of motions. What makes sameness certain in scientific work?

> If we experiment twice, do the differences between the two occasions make them different experiments or only different instances of the same experiment, the answer . . . is always relative to a theory – we cannot repeat an experiment and look for a covering theory; we must have at least a partial theory before we know whether we have a repetition of the experiment. (Goodman, 1972, p. 439)

The fourth stricture is that similarity does not explain metaphor or metaphorical truth. Rather the other way round, the practice of referring to two objects metaphorically constitutes their similarity.

> Metaphorical use may serve to explain the similarity better than – or at least as well as – the similarity explains the metaphor. (Goodman, 1972, p. 440)

The fifth and sixth strictures are to do with induction and although they are very relevant to the inductions we make as anthropologists about the principles governing other cultures, I make bold to leave them aside in the present context. Already to accept the first four strictures would be for anthropologists a severe curtailment of our usual interpretive activities. The only comfort is that similarity depends on use, on a habit, a practice, a theory however small or a hypothesis however implicit, that picks out the common properties that are held to constitute similarity. If the anthropologist can locate the foreign theory that entrenches a foreign metaphor, and if the theory can be shown to be actually used by the foreigners for prediction, production or remedy, then his interpretation is on safe ground. Otherwise he is probably abusing similarity by making it do more work than it can perform.

This adds up to saying that an interpretation based on discerning a match between one set of things and its representation needs some further guarantee. Metaphors are no more natural phenomena than anomalies. To escape the reproach of having been too imaginative, the anthropologist needs to do more. First, the foreign metaphor has to have local testimony that this is what it means to the foreigner. Then there is the quality of that testimony: is it just one person who said so, or is there some evidence for the wider use of the metaphor; and is the usage a one-off lyrical moment in a poet's rhapsody, or is it institutionalized as part of the regular habits of the people, a resemblance picked out by their theories of the world and their hypotheses?

All three requirements were met by Turner's (1962) analysis of whiteness metaphors in Ndembu culture. Why can we believe him when he says that for the Ndembu the whiteness of milk resembles the white sap of a certain tree, and that whiteness of both and whiteness in general means matrilineal descent and continuity? We accept these metaphors not merely because he can quote and name his

Ndembu instructors. He witnessed the uses to which the metaphors were put in ceremonies that deployed the redness of blood and of red saps of trees, and the blackness of charcoal and of bile. But important evidence of the institutionalizing of the meanings of the colours is in his account of the social alignments in clans and villages. His interpretation of the metaphors depends upon their use in ceremonies that act the part of theories in upholding perceptions of similarity. Their explanations of the causes of barrenness, sickness and death are indeed theories in which the metaphors are entrenched with consistency at many different levels.

The example is all the better for my purpose because Turner did incautiously let go of these safeguards of his interpretation and tried to find Ndembu meanings of whiteness in other cultures (1962) and, needless to say, found them and got to be duly criticized for it. In situations where there are no guarantees against subjective recognition of similarity, the searcher will always find what he seeks.

I freely confess that in *Natural Symbols* (1970) I wrote as if the interpretation of the metaphor must be right if it can be shown to correspond to the social structure. But my perception of the social structure as being like that of the symbolic order is a resemblance that I have picked out. It also needs anchorage. Goodman says that correspondence never carries its own guarantee; the match between the symbolic system and the social system is a similarity that I perceive, but of itself it cannot confirm the interpretation that matches them up. Alas, Goodman's strictures on the abuse of similarity undo this interpretive complacency. First, they apply to the recognition of any pattern as being similar to something else, since similarity is not a quality that inheres in things. When we recognize the social

130

system as the same from one year to the next, we are again invoking similarity; but now we know that similarity is not a quality of things. The matching features of the social system between one visit and the next have to be selected by the viewer as in any other similarity case. Just to see the same social arrangements continuing between two visits involves backgrounding the changes or overlooking them altogether.

Ignorant of these snares, I have attributed to the ancient Israelites a metaphorical construction that makes table, altar and marriage bed into analogies one with another, and also temple, nation and human body, and I have used the larger structure of analogy to explain animal categories prohibited in the Mosaic dietary code (Douglas, 1975a). If all these interpretations have to be sent back to the drawing board because we start to take Goodman seriously, so also must be many other interpretations of animal symbols. No names, no pack drill: I name no names, but remark only that I am in good company. The case for animal metaphors is no weaker and no stronger than the case for metaphors found in hair, food and sex.

Another favourite interpretive ploy is an even worse case: that is the promise to show that symbolic forms are inverted images of social reality (see the discussion of inversion with regard to folklore in Chapter 1). First there is the questionable identifying of enduring images in the symbolism; secondly, there is the challengeable identifying of enduring patterns in social behaviour; thirdly, there is the dubious alleged resemblance between the symbolic pattern and the pattern of society. Fourthly, there is the even more difficult identifying of an inverse pattern of an image; then the alleged enduring inverse pattern of social reality, and last, there is more trouble with the claimed match between the two inverted images.

One attempt to escape from the similarity strictures and other doubts is to throw all the metaphors into the air at once; set the wheel of lights turning, and make such a virtuoso dazzle that everyone will succumb to the irresistible pattern of patterns reflecting one another. This method is used brilliantly by Geertz (1973) in his account of Balinese cockfighting. Reading it, criticism is seduced by each new facet of resemblance that is brought into the play of matching metaphors. For example the cock which the man watching the cockfight is holding between his knees is a metaphorical penis. In themselves umpteen extra facets of metaphor do not improve the analysis of the cockfight's meaning; their alleged coherence, because it depends on notions of similarity, comes under the strictures like the rest. Claimed coherence between metaphors is a good sign of the investigator's perseverance and ingenuity; trying to demonstrate it is a spur to improve the evidence. But of itself coherence between numerous metaphors cannot justify an argument. Something more is needed.

Following Ryle (1949), Geertz has called this method of pursing the ethnographer's avocation 'thick description', an attempt to get at 'the sort of piled up structures of inference and implication through which an ethnographer is continually trying to pick his way' (Geertz, 1973, p. 7). As the meanings of the people being studied are thickly interleaved, so does the ethnographer's skill have to be as subtle in uncovering the various layers. The power of this form of reporting to carry conviction depends on showing coherence between multiple contexts.

There is a difference between Ryle's and Geertz's use of the idea of thick description. For Ryle it is used critically in a philosophical argument about what the everyday processes of interpretation involve. Geertz is using it prescriptively to help ethnographers to describe what other people's meanings are. Both are wary of imputing too much intellectual theorizing to the agents who are the subject of study. Geertz is deeply wary of the kind of theorizing that codifies abstract regularities and seeks to generalize even to the point of creating a fantasy world of academic satisfaction that has no correspondence with ethnographic realities. For him the essential task of theory-building is to make thick description possible, generalizing within cases and not across them (Geertz, 1973, p. 26) and then gradually to build up an understanding about how cultural processes work. He is not trying to do without theory, but he likes it to be modest and secure in its micro-foundations.

Geertz is very explicit that he is not recommending thick description as a method to replace established techniques of gathering information. It is rather an outcome or objective. If he were proffering the rich concatenation of metaphors that he deploys as a method of ethnography he would be vulnerable to the charge of resting explanation on similarity. The strictures do not apply if thickness of description be sought with enough attention to the intentions that have been framed by institutional supports that coordinate and steady the meanings, but we the observers have to catalogue them and assess them. We also have to justify our interpretations of the metaphors, and here again, similarity does not pick out replicas or icons. We also depend on theories and institutional habits for our interpretations. Though I fully share Geertz's preference for small theories tried and working at microlevels, I am sure that it is much better that they be made explicit.

The temptation to let resemblance do the work of explanation is strong because coherence of metaphors works very well as an interpretive rule within one culture.

Remember that similarity is culture-dependent. Similarity has explanatory power within our own culture, based as it has to be upon shared similarity perceptions. Statements of similarity 'are still serviceable in the streets' (Goodman, 1972, p. 446), but they do not help us to go from one culture to another.

On this line of argument, if fieldwork reports have problems with metaphors, so much the more does mythology. Nothing can stave off doubts about the interpretation of metaphor in purely literary uses. In some genres there are verbal equivalents to the supporting institutional structures that safeguard Turner's Ndembu interpretations. For example, though there is plenty of cause for scepticism about my interpretation of the Mosaic dietary rules, this is in fact much more secure just because it is about rules to be observed and therefore about concepts and theories expected to be in use in a more practical way than stories can ever be. Narrative has problems about symbolization and literary solutions of its own that do not help with interpreting anthropological materials about symbols in use and I regret to say that I do not think that the literary analysis, bound as it is to representational models of interpretation, can be helped by the viewpoint that I am developing here. (See Chapter 1.)

Returning to Goodman's strictures, since similarity is culture-bound, our need is to develop our culture of anthropological interpretation. And since similarity does not pick out icons, since similarity of itself gives no guarantees of interpretation, no method based solely on representational theory will help. The theory has to be one that systematically links behaviour to interpretation; it has to be a theory of behaviour.

For lack of discussion of method and theory the

materials that are collected in
Central African fieldwork
about animal symbolism
remain very disparate. The
Lele take a special interest
in the lesser scaly antea-
ter or tree pangolin
(Figure 6.1). They used
to make it the object of a
fertility cult. I have
described it (1957, p. 50)
as anomalous in their
system of classification on
the basis of their descriptions
of its habits and habitat,
supplemented by knowledge
of the rites they perform when
they catch one and eat it, and
by their theories of sickness
and health. I would like to
know whether neighbouring
peoples whose forest it inha-
bits also regard it as a fish-like
mammalian tree-climber, one
of the most powerful nature
spirits in their world, giver of
fertility and good hunting.

Figure 6.1   *Tree pangolin*
(drawn by Pat Novy)

Roberts (1986) and Thomas Blakeley (personal communication) have worked for a long time among the
Tabwa, who live north and east of the Lele. The Tabwa
also know of the pangolin and use its scales in medicine,
but they pay less attention to the animal than they do to
another ant-eating animal, the aardvark. In their mythology they are said to treat the aardvark as a heroic human

135

surrogate, but I have explained why mythological material unsupported by practice and theory is a poor support for interpretation. Tabwa practice clearly does support the claim that the aardvark is regarded by the Tabwa as an anomalous beast: its long sensitive snout reminds them of a penis; when they kill it the hunters try not to let the women see it, because of their derisive laughter at the obscenely excessive sexuality of a creature with a penis at each end. Tabwa are reported to have no rituals at all about the aardvark. Most of my information about Lele attitudes to pangolins comes from dietary rules and behaviour, and I have no Lele myths about either pangolin or aardvark. To the best of my knowledge the Lele regard the aardvark as a rather unimpressive burrowing animal, of timid disposition, with hind legs too weak to run and a funny snout. It could be that there is much more similarity between the Lele and the Tabwa animal symbolism, but the very different interests of the various investigators make attempts at comparison pointless.

I am left with no comparable materials about animal symbolism in other parts of Central Africa, since my closest colleagues working in the vicinity are, respectively, specialists in history, mythology, ethnoscience and symbolism, but none is really interested in food habits and dietary regulations. It is possible, but I think implausible, that the Lele are unique in their complex of rules prohibiting different kinds of animal meats to different social categories. Goody (1982, pp. 38, 97) plays down the social symbolism of food in Africa compared with Europe and Asia, but among the Lele it expresses category distinctions of a more specialized kind, between male and female, child and adult, living and dead, religious initiates and lay folk. By mapping out the human categories and the animal categories, and noting the rules that connected them, I was able to draw diagrams that showed the animal kinds as projections of human society (1975b, p. 299). It was really quite easy and to me aesthetically satisfying. I expected the similarity of the two pictures to compel assent. But now that I know that similarity of itself does not pick out icons or replicas I have to think through the knowledge that resemblance does not guarantee interpretation. Taking aboard the full lesson that similarity cannot bear explanatory weight, I try to look at the material again.

In the summer of 1988 I returned to Zaire and revisited the Lele after a very long absence. Everything was changed. Christianization had driven the old religion underground; intense animosity between Christians and the rest was manifested in reciprocal accusations of sorcery; the pangolin cult was outlawed, its prohibitions a matter of fun for the Christians and of embarrassment for the believers. Furthermore, the depletion of the forest and of its fauna meant that no one now saw many of the animals that formerly figured on the regular menu. Consequently I was able to be told things about the animals that were initiates' secrets before. For example, I learnt that the pangolin's long ant-eating tongue is rooted at the top of the spine and holds the ribs in place. This gives it a tremendous advantage against sorcery, which attacks the lungs of victims, for its tongue anchors its ribs so that they can never come adrift from the spine as human ribs are thought to do, causing chest pains and coughing and death. A longer visit would elicit more of such wonderful information about individual animals. I learnt that the initiated diviners are forbidden to eat the Nile monitor because of its spotted skin and, as I began to get a list of prohibitions on other spotted animals, I found a whole theoretical field about the nature spirits and their interest in spottedness and a class of skin diseases that includes smallpox. Inevitably a concern with the classification of animals and humans leads to local theories about life and death whose outcomes are shown in the menus and food rules. The theories sustain the classification and give meaning to the metaphors. Getting at their theories allows the investigator to bypass representational theories of cognition and so to avoid the strictures on misuse of similarity. But how do we get at their theories? Not by deducing them from the metaphors.

In the late 1980s, after numerous philosophers have insisted that sameness is not a property of things, the idea that animal categories serve primarily as an abstract model of human society appears to be very questionable. My argument is that the animal categories come up in the same patterns of relations as those of humans because the said humans understand the animal kinds to be acting according to the same principles as they themselves. On this approach the humans, that is the foreigners whom anthropologists report in ethnography, are using cognitive economy. They are not using animals for drawing elaborate pictures of themselves, nor are they necessarily using them for posing and answering profound metaphysical problems. The argument is that they have practical reasons for trying to understand and predict the animal's ways, reasons to do with health and hygiene and sickness. The principles of seniority, marriage exchange, territory, and political hegemony that they use for explaining their own behaviour they also use for predictions about animal behaviour. It is a very economical argument depending on low-level micro-observation and modest theory, and more plausible than the theory of a projection of human society upon nature.

We can accept the idea that humans need to think out

their difference from animals and that animal differentia-
tions are a splendidly apt source of metaphors for thinking
about human differentiation without accepting the idea
that a well-matched differentiated animal world is essentially a resource for thinking about ourselves. Rather the
other way round, how could we think about how animals
relate to one another except on the basis of our own
relationships?

This is not to question the iconicity of an animal model
of the human world. We can question that mirroring
society is its primary use. And we can be interested in how
it gets to be constructed. I suggest that there is a more
fundamental, non-metaphorical kind of connection
between the way humans think of themselves and how
they think of animals. Once this other way is established,
metaphors flourish upon its basis. The argument does not
question Lévi-Strauss's (1962) idea that 'animals are good
to think'. It merely supposes that totemic schemes are not
essentially metaphoric constructions, or rather than, in so
far as they are interpretable as mirror images of human
society, this will be because their categories have already
been set up in the same patterns as the categories of
human social relations. This is a variant of Horton's (1967)
idea that in African traditional thought 'the mind in quest
of explanatory analogies turns naturally to people and
their relations'.

The similarity that we observe between the two spheres,
human and animal, would result from the fact that both
spheres are constructed upon the same principles. That the
model of the animal world turns out to look so like that of
the human world would be a byproduct of native theory
about how animal society is constituted. The liberating
idea that comes from taking Goodman and the other
philosophers on similarity seriously is that there has not

been so much picture-making in primitive thought as theorizing and not so much philosophy as reflection on practical issues; the models are derived from an immediate concern to figure out how the world works and concern to frame the classifications that work best with acceptable theory.

Briefly, Lele categorize humans and teach them how to behave with equals, seniors and juniors according to whether the relations come under the principles that govern the friendship or enmity of equals, or the principles of seniority and patronage. Equals, that is friends or enemies, recognize no territorial or property constraints. Patron–client relations have a strong territorial aspect. Client–client relations under the same patron entail mutual honour and respect. The practical issue is to know what is safe to eat.

If they want to understand why some animals of very different species share the same habitat peacefully, they apply their ideas of patron–client relations because it is a case of shared territory: if they want to understand the aggressive behaviour of carnivores they apply their ideas of enmity. By the same token, animals that cohabit in the territory of nature spirits are assumed to be clients of the spirits. The peaceful cohabitation of fish, lizards, water snakes and wild boar in the streams implies that they have secured the protection of the water spirits and have become their clients; on the human model this means that the spirits will avenge aggression against their clients, so it will not be safe to eat them if one is in alliance with a water spirit.

The model they use assumes a common set of intentions and reactions, as between humans and spirits, and between spirits and animals. If a Lele enters a clientship relation with a water spirit or if, as often happens, the spirit has made a pact of friendship with a human, the usual respect from co-clients or towards friends' clients will be exacted. When humans enter into relations of clientship with various animals and spirits they do not prey on their non-human co-clients any more than they would on co-clients of a human overlord. To prey on co-clients would incur the anger of the patron. So it is not safe to eat animals indicated by rules that govern their own daily social life as co-clients of a common patron. Observing the intricate rules about what an individual human can eat or not eat with safety among animal species has a strong practical interest. The daily menu, which differentiates categories of humans by their diet sheet, is the surface appearance of deep theory about life and death and health and sickness.

If this is a plausible explanation of how Lele think about animal kinds, it is also a small but powerful theory about how other people think about the animal kinds that they have constructed. As a method it suggests that minute attention be paid to how animals interact with humans and to the interests that humans pursue when they chase or eat or tame animals or harness them to work. It is a method for establishing meanings that escapes the strictures on similarity. It explains the theorizing by which the classes of animal kinds are put together, but I should emphasize that it does not necessarily undermine extant analyses of animal symbols based on attributed metaphorical meanings. These always have to contend with the strictures on similarity unless a purely literary, even fictional, account is required.

The difficulties inherent in arguments based on similarity provide plenty of reason for worry for the structural analysis of myth and for the quantities of symbolic similarities that have been perceived in anthropology since Lévi-Strauss's publication in 1962 of *La Pensée sauvage* (*The*

Savage Mind, 1966). My own emphasis on practical reasoning about society as the basis for the systems of metaphors called totemism is actually anticipated very specifically in Radcliffe-Brown (1952, p. 130), when he said that:

> For the primitive the universe as a whole is a moral or social order governed not by what we call natural law but rather by what we must call moral or ritual law . . . In Australia, for example, there are innumerable ways in which the natives have built up between themselves and the phenomena of nature a system of relations which are essentially similar to the relations that they have built up in their social structure between one human being and another.

In the last few pages of *The Savage Mind* Lévi-Strauss emphasizes the underlying practical basis of primitive thought and its uses of marriage relations for models (1966, p. 265). The difference that he sees between savage thought and ours does not lie in greater mystical or contemplative propensities on their side, but in our practice of disengaging our various metaphors from the matrix of social relations and dealing with them in fragments.

What I am proposing, then, is very much in the mainstream, with the only difference that this time it is not an idea but a method of research. My method is proposed as a remedy, a supplement, a way of establishing meanings by reference to use, a control on the imagination of the researcher. However, nothing much more can be said about proving or disproving the argument I am making unless ethnographic material is gathered with this theory in mind. Its merit is to answer a peculiarly Anglo-Saxon curiosity about the mechanisms of symbolic thinking. Lévi-Strauss's theory of totemism is sometimes presented as humanity brooding on itself and its place in nature. His emphasis on the contemplative interests is certainly there: '[t]his reciprocity of perspectives, in which man and the world mirror each other and which seems to us the only possible explanation of the properties and capacities of the savage mind' (Lévi-Strauss, 1966, p. 222).

But the whole strategy of his argument was to relate the classifications of nature to the classifications of kinship and marriage. The mirror effect that we discern is the result of the process that I am writing about, a process whose study I suggest is an appropriate method for research on animal symbolism. It may be lack of imagination, but for some it is difficult to imagine humanity brooding on its identity and on its separation from animality or to accept the love of philosophic contemplation as the explanation of the consistency of so-called savage thought. In Genesis we have no special difficulty with the idea that God brooded over the waters because everything to do with divinity is mysterious, but how does humanity contemplate or consider? What mysterious mechanism sets up the initial categories?

According to the method I propose, we do not have to assume any such thing. Animals are brought into human social categories by a simple extension to them of the principles that serve for ordering human relationships. The method is to do the painstaking work of tracking how the categories are used.

References

Bulmer, R. (1986) *The Unsolved Problems of the Birds of Leviticus.* Auckland: University of Auckland Working Papers in Anthropology.

Douglas, M. (1957) 'Animals in Lele religious symbolism', *Africa* 27(1): 46–58.

Douglas, M. (1966) *Purity and Danger: an Analysis of Concepts of Pollution and Taboo.* London: Routledge & Kegan Paul.

Douglas, M. (1970) *Natural Symbols, Explorations in Cosmology.* London: Penguin.

Thought styles

Douglas, M. (1975a) 'Deciphering a meal', in M. Douglas, *Implicit Meanings*. London: Routledge & Kegan Paul. pp. 249–75.

Douglas, M. (1975b) 'Self-evidence', in M. Douglas, *Implicit Meanings*. London: Routledge & Kegan Paul. pp. 276–318.

Geertz, C. (1973) *The Interpretation of Cultures*. New York: Basic Books.

Goodman, N. (1972) *Problems and Projects*. New York: Bobbs Merrill.

Goody, J. (1982) *Cooking, Cuisine and Class: a Study in Comparative Sociology*. Cambridge: Cambridge University Press.

Horton, R. (1967) 'African traditional thought and Western science', *Africa*, 37(1&2): 50–7, 155–87.

Lévi-Strauss, C. (1962) (1964 trans. R. Needham) *Totemism*. London: Merlin Press.

Lévi-Strauss, C. (1966 [1962]) *The Savage Mind*. London: Weidenfeld & Nicolson.

Radcliffe-Brown, A.R. (1952 [1929]) 'The sociological theory of totemism', in A.R. Radcliffe-Brown, *Structure and Function in Primitive Society*. London: Cohen & West. pp. 117–32.

Roberts, A. (1986) 'Social and historical contexts of Tabwa art', in A. Roberts and E. Maurer (eds), *The Rising of a New Moon: a Century of Tabwa Art*. Seattle: University of Washington Press. pp. 1–48.

Ryle, G. (1949) *The Concept of Mind*. New York: Barnes & Noble.

Turner, V.W. (1962) *Chishamba, the White Spirit*. Rhodes-Livingstone Paper 33. Manchester: Manchester University Press.

7

Classified as Edible

Bulmer's proximity principle

In his original study of how Karam classify birds and animals, Ralph Bulmer showed that a few simple principles could account for the main divisions. The principles were based on a human-centred view of the world in which other beings were classed according to their degree of remoteness from the human domain (Bulmer, 1967). His essay on the puzzling list of birds which the Bible prohibits as unclean applied these principles again (Bulmer, 1986). With full attention to the difficulty of identifying the birds by their Hebrew names, and with attention to the textual problems, he tried to study the birds' habitats, their feeding and nesting, their degree of remoteness from human dwellings and whether they stayed within their natural boundaries or invaded human habitation. He was using proximity from human life as a taxonomic dimension for other people's classification.

Broadly speaking and with due allowance for guess-work, his proximity principle seems to work for the Book of Leviticus:

> Thus the list starts with birds that dominate the sky and dwell in high places, remote from human settlement, past or present. It then shifts focus, to those with primary association with waste land, remote from current human settlement but, especially, characterised by ruined cities and land made desolate by war. And it concludes with creatures that, with

almost uncanny disregard for human beings, occupy or invade farmland and habitations . . . All those birds, and most other wild creatures that are designated in Leviticus as unclean, not merely deviate from the ideal vegetarian diet [reference to Genesis 1: 30] but variously challenge man's lordship over nature. (Bulmer, 1986, p. 23)

The conclusion is that Leviticus's list of birds reveals a strong ordering based on degrees of proximity to human life and only a weak ordering based on groupings of species and genera.

In this conclusion he was commenting on extensive scholarship which has supposed that the Israelites were first prohibited from eating blood and secondly from eating carnivorous animals and carrion eaters because of the blood in their diet. He argued that the dietary habits of the birds were not distinctive enough to warrant such a notion; if the rule is to pick out and prohibit carnivorous birds, too large a number of birds beyond those listed are carnivorous, without counting worms and insects as meat. He deals effectively with the other theories that have been proposed.

The idea of natural kinds plays two roles in his paper. First there is the zoological concept of kinds distinguished as species and genera. Then there is the related concept of an 'avian norm' based on distribution of particular species in a region. Some birds deviate conspicuously from the culturally defined avian norm, and so, as they attract the attention of taxonomers, they come to be rated unclean or abnormal while animals that conform to the norm tend to be regarded as clean or normal. This idea of deviation from the norm was important in his thinking. He hoped to find that across the world the naturally deviant kinds, such as big wingless birds or flying fish, would be universally treated as culturally deviant and therefore as unclean or

146

the equivalent. In this way he would surprise anthropologists by uncovering a universal cultural principle
(Bulmer, personal communication). However, the information about the Levitical list of birds was too sketchy and
too unreliable to encourage him in this line of thought.
Both these arguments, the norm and the deviations from
the norm, require that the characteristics of the animals or
birds are more or less self-classifying, their deviations from
their normal distribution provoke the human response. In
that model, the culture is relatively passive, the active
principle is in the characteristics of nature. The animals'
peculiarities strike the observers, hit them in the eye as it
were. This I find a very doubtful claim.

However, his other argument is much better. That is that
each community constructs its natural kinds of birds, on
the basis of human use, and the birds' distance from and
invasiveness of human habitation, in short, the proximity
principle. This is a stronger idea than may at first be
apparent and it deserves to be taken seriously in the plans
for future ethno-zoological research. It calls for a much
more thorough-going attempt to relate the social organization and technology and the cultural values of the bird
watchers to their classifying activity.

In the principle of proximity Bulmer had hit on a
generalization which can be tested out in different cultures.
Implicitly it is part of a theory about the transformation of
human attention as it moves away from a centre of activity
and about the shifts in the organized perception of animal
kinds that follow the movement from centre to periphery.
To go any further with that insight we would need to
develop the theory. There is a regrettable tendency in
anthropology to treat folk classification as a separate com-
partment of our interests. Consequently, to make the point
emphatically, I will need to produce all the argumentative

persuasion I can muster. The study of folk taxonomy has to be purged of ethnocentric assumptions about similarity. What we take to be similar properties will only haphazardly correspond to what is taken to be similar by other peoples. It is equally pointless to look for what we perceive to be anomalies in animal behaviour as a clue to why given classes of animals get special treatment. In what follows I will widen the field of argument.

Resemblance is not a property

Of course we know that categories which put things together in the same class are entirely the work of rational minds, invented by them for the sake of discourse and action. Bulmer's proximity principle draws attention to something about the discourse, a criterion of distance between speakers and the objects spoken about. In his hands it also says a lot more about the kind of interaction that is going on between the speakers and the objects they speak about. The interaction gives a frame of reference. In living and working together and speaking together about their work, the persons are making their world. They are actively defining themselves and the rest. Their role is not passive; objects don't shout out what class they belong in, properties don't jump out and announce their similarities. The human agents who are inventing strong ordering processes for their lives are ordering themselves at the same time, and ordering their world.

The frame of reference puts the objects into the categories. To understand how the folk classification works we would therefore need to know the frames of reference, and not just to know them singly, frame by frame, but as a system that is a working version of the world. Nelson Goodman's epistemology emphasizes the process of worldmaking, that is, the ongoing cognitive process of revising versions of the world (Goodman, 1978). Within a particular cultural scheme things are defined as being the same if they belong to the same set. If things show the necessary criteria for belonging to the set, they have a shared identity, a resemblance. For ethno-science the question is how the things get into the set in the first place. Does their common identity depend on their belonging to it, or does belonging to the set depend on their having the same common properties? Defining similarity by belonging to the set and defining the set by the similarity of its members is circular. The circle cannot be broken by reaching out for physical, bedrock sources of sameness. Any two things whatever, as disparate as you like on some criteria (such as the camel and the rock badger classed in one set in Leviticus 11), can be counted the same by selecting shared features. There are an infinite number of good reasons for assigning any two things to the same set (Goodman, 1969). Being similar is an endowment of intellectual activity, which necessarily has to start with sets, categories, classes. But the intellectual activity articulates the rest of behaviour, and the clues as to what is going on are in that behaviour.

If anthropologists tend to think that similarity speaks for itself, they are not alone. The cognitive psychologist Amos Tversky (1977) defines similarity as a function of common and distinctive features weighted for salience or importance. But weighting here means selecting, and he takes it for granted that it is not necessary to say how the selecting of features is done. As Murphy and Medin (1985) ask, in a useful review of assumptions about similarity recognition in psychology, what are we to count as a feature? Between plums and lawn mowers, the list of similar features could be infinite. The answer is that the framework elicits features that will be treated as similar. At the beginning of scientific theorizing ambiguous entities abound (Quine, 1969). The initial questions are:

Is it a cocoon?
Is it a caterpillar?
Is it a butterfly?
Are they several kinds of creatures as their appearance would suggest, or are they the same one in meta-morphosis?

Instead the biologist asks something like:

Are they part of a system?
How does it work?
What larger system is it part of?

With full theoretical development, ambiguities and problems of identification disappear. When problems of identity appear it is because of an inadequate embracing scheme within which the classified item functions.

In science the problems of classifying are solved by theoretical frameworks. In everyday life regular activities create a framework of expectations, much as theory does for science. In society the institutional framework does the same. Or it may be helpful to use the metaphor of language. In a spoken phrase, the elements of the verbal sequence are held in place by the grammar. If there were no such ordering principle, there would be no basis for sense, so ambiguity and uncertainty about meaning would be manifest. The ordering principle – whatever it may be – is all important.

James Mill's contribution

Once taken aboard that the frame of reference makes the classes and bestows on objects co-classified their qualities of similarity, a fundamental problem is solved. Can there be a recognition of sameness prior to the ordering principle that assigns items to sets? James Mill decided no, and he was right. He was struck by this problem when he launched the nineteenth-century debate about mental association. Picking up the theme from Hobbes and Hume, he said:

> Mr. Hume, and after him other philosophers, have said that our ideas are associated according to three principles, Contiguity in time and place, Causation and Resemblance. The contiguity in time and place must mean that of the sensations, and so far as it is affirmed that the order of the ideas follows that of the sensations, contiguity of two sensations in time means the successive order. Contiguity of two sensations in place means the synchronous order . . . Causation is only the name for the order established between an antecedent and a consequent . . . (1869, p. 106)

Then, immediately after this, he questioned whether resemblance has any claim to equal status with contiguity, decided that it has not and that it is therefore not to be counted as a law of mental association:

> Resemblance only remains, as an alleged principle of association, and it is necessary to enquire whether it is included in the laws which have been expounded. I believe that we are accustomed to see like things together. When we see a tree, we generally see more trees than one; a sheep, more sheep than one; a man, more men than one. From this observation, I think, we may refer resemblance to the law of frequency, of which it seems to form only a particular case.

His rejection of the principle of resemblance as part of the laws of mental association might have been the end of the matter. Similarity would have been relegated to the secondary place he gave it, and along with similarity, dissimilarity and anomaly too. However, his editor and

151

son, John, questioned the bold conclusion and claimed to have refuted the idea that similarity can be reduced to contiguity, in two very lengthy footnotes (1869, pp. 112–13, 121–6).

William James called Mill the elder's repudiation of resemblance as a principle of association 'assuredly one of the curiosities of literature' (1890, p. 600) and reproduced in full the statement just quoted. William James hedged on the issue. On the one hand he insisted that similarity is no elementary law and that there is no elementary causal law of association other than the 'law of neural habit' (1890, p. 566), which sounds as if he agrees with James Mill. On the other hand, he still agreed with 'the immense majority of contemporary psychologists [who] retained both Resemblance and Contiguity as irreducible principles of Association'.

Structural analysis

If William James instead of repudiating it had added his authority to the view of James Mill a lot of head-scratching and spilt ink would have been saved. That there are two distinct mental laws, similarity and contiguity, has proved a very seductive idea, with prima facie appeal but fundamental difficulties (Benson, 1979). James Frazer (1890) proposed them as the two principles of magical thought. Henri Bergson (1896) distinguished two forms of cognitive disorder, one in which old images cannot be recalled and one in which the connecting link between perception and movement is broken. He implied that there are two kinds of cognitive process, one which recognizes images by likeness, and one which depends on an ordering principle. Roman Jakobson (1966) took up the same theme in teaching that there are two kinds of speech disorder, one the failure of the capacity to match words to sense, the other the failure of contiguity, of the power to organize words. This encouraged in linguistics and anthropology and in structuralist theory a succession of researchers attempting to make the distinction convincingly. Some have admitted their difficulty in making out which is which. Others have glossed it over, rightly confident that the similarity of a class of objects can usually be recognized by the readers, thanks to their shared habits (Lévi-Strauss, 1955). Because this practice assumes that their interpretations are within a common culture, it is of no use for ethnoscience.

The difficulty comes from confusing two levels of classification. Seen as part of an activity at the practical level of everyday life, objects come to us carrying their own classifications and similar properties. At the next level, logic starts from classes which have already been made. John Stuart Mill writing his dissenting footnote to his father's work was writing on logic, but James Mill was considering the pre-logical question of how things are sorted into classes. He was aware that things cannot be organized differently and still be the same things. The thingness that makes them recognizable as members of a class depends on the organization to which they are subjected.

Facts and theories

The reason why many clever people have clung to the notion of similarity or resemblance as an independent principle, on a par with contiguity, was that contiguity itself was too thin a notion to be worthy of carrying the load of explanation. To explain the workings of the mind by mere succession, mere habit, was not only unconvincing, it was disturbing. There had to be something else, and in fact there is: that missing something is organization, a frame of reference, concerted activity, theories about the world that make sense of interaction. If we ask what makes any two things contiguous in our experience, the answer is usually some form of activity. The way the activity is organized creates the contiguities and these support the sense of similarity. The contrast between theory and fact is not a contrast between two different elements, but between two inextricably mixed parts of a process.

The master detectives

At the turn of the century the theory of mental association suddenly fell into the lap of the short-story writers and begot a new literary genre. The detective story was originally strongly based on popular ideas of the latent presence in the mind of unconsciously received impressions and on free association deliberately used to drag them out of their latency. In 'The Vindictive Story of the Footsteps that Ran' (Sayers, 1945) Peter Wimsey is lunching with a young doctor, and is drawing a parallel between medical diagnosis and photography:

> 'One hears a thing or sees it without knowing or thinking about it, and it all comes back, and one sorts out one's impressions. Like those plates of Bunter's. Picture all there, la-la-, what's the word I want Bunter?'
>
> 'Latent, my lord.'
>
> 'That's it, my right hand man, Bunter. Couldn't do a thing without him. The picture's latent till you put the developer on. Same thing with the brain.'

At this point a man rushes in, his wife has been murdered in the kitchen upstairs, the criminal escaped through the kitchen window while the husband was in the sitting room; he suspects her Italian lover. They search; no weapon is to be seen; the wound suggests something six inches long and narrow, the Constable supposes a stiletto. Lord Peter examines the kitchen thoroughly and pores over the signs of preparing a Sunday dinner. The kitchen is hot, the oven is still on. Bunter and he talk about how facts are selected by theories:

> 'Dr. Hartman has a theory. In any investigation, my Bunter, it is damnable dangerous to have a theory.'
> 'I have heard you say so, my lord.'
> 'Confound you – you know it as well as I do! What is wrong with the doctor's theories, Bunter?'
> 'You wish me to reply that he only sees the facts which fit in with the theory.'
> 'Thought reader!' exclaimed Lord Peter bitterly.
> 'And that he supplies them to the police, my lord.'

A little later Wimsey approaches the doctor himself.

> 'Dr. Hartman, something is wrong. Cast your mind back. We were talking about symptoms. Then came the scream. Then came the sound of feet running. Which direction did they run?'
> 'I am sure I don't know.'
> 'Don't you? Symptomatic, though, doctor. They have been troubling me all the time, subconsciously. Now I know why. They ran *from* the kitchen.'

After this, further clues emerge which lay suspicion on the husband who had said that he ran into the kitchen. But no one knows how he did the murder. Again alone with Bunter, Wimsey tries to work out what it was they had observed in the kitchen . . . something there had been wrong. What was it? Bunter says:

> 'I could not say, my lord, but I entertain a conviction that I was also, in a manner of speaking, conscious – not consciously-conscious, my lord, if you understand me, but still conscious of an incongruity.'

155

They then go over all the details of the kitchen. Peter reminisces in free association about his childhood recollections of watching a cook prepare a chicken for the oven. The thought strikes them both simultaneously: the dripping which should have greased the bird had not been touched. So the bird had been put in the oven only half prepared.

> 'Bunter! Suppose it was never put in till after she was dead: thrust in hurriedly by somebody who had something to hide? Horrible!'
> 'But with what object, my lord?'
> 'Yes, why? That is the point. One more mental association with the bird. It's just coming. Wait a moment. Pluck, draw, wash, stuff, tuck up, truss – By God!'

Peter Wimsey rushes to the oven door, pulls out the half cooked bird stuck with the six inch skewer. No wonder the husband's footsteps were running the wrong way. He had not been in the sitting room as he had claimed but in the kitchen.

The story illustrates the principle of contiguity and the way that it is used in interpretation. The order in which things should have happened if the account is true is measured against the order of noises heard and physical traces. Two organizing schemes are matched for discrepancies: one, the everyday routine of cooking, which would have produced one sequence of events; the other, the order which produced the murder.

Detective fiction made much more creative use of the idea of mental association than the psychologists. The difference between facts and theories were their regular stock in trade. 'Nothing is so deceptive as an obvious fact', said Sherlock Holmes in the 'Boscombe Valley Mystery' (Conan Doyle, 1892). G.K. Chesterton's Father Brown often

156

insisted that familiarity blinds the eye, as here in 'The Song of the Fish' (1927):

> 'A thing can sometimes be too close to be seen, as for instance, a man cannot see himself . . . If something is in the fore-ground of our life we hardly see it, and if we did, we might think it quite odd . . . '
>
> 'Jameson was so dull and colourless that I forgot all about him.'
>
> 'Beware of the man you forget', said Father Brown, 'He is the man who has you entirely at a disadvantage.'

From the 1890s the writers of detective fiction elaborated upon the theory of mental association. First the master detective had deliberately to use techniques of dissociation to free his own mental processes from the channels of previously established associations. So Sherlock Holmes used opium and music; Father Brown believed in sleep and prayer; Peter Wimsey cultivated a number of hobbies, such as photography and expertise in wine, which by their diversity prevented his mind from following the obvious paths; Knox's Bredon played long games of patience; Christie's Poirot slept to refresh the little grey cells. Then they were ready to uncover the simulacra organized by the minds of the master criminals. They were not deceived by similarities. Similarity in itself was never enough for them; they looked for the organizing principle, and this meant searching for the intentions of their subjects. Facts were despised or suspect.

Though footsteps may leave a clear negative imprint, like the fossil elephant in the rock, or the silver salt cellar in its velvet lined case, in themselves the physical traces are just facts; they say very little. We need to observe what direction the steps are going, as Wimsey observed in the case of the skewered wife above, or whether they are walking or running, as Father Brown observed in the case of 'The Jewelled Fish Knives' when the master criminal impersonated alternately a guest in the restaurant by walking slowly, and a waiter by hurrying. We are warned not to jump to conclusions based on the direction in which the feet are pointing, as when Bredon noticed that the wet prints of a naked foot on the steps of a bridge were made by walking up backwards (Knox, 1928). Why would anyone ever do that?

Conclusion

The early master detectives went far beyond the psychologists in assuming that neither similarity nor contiguity in themselves reveal the truth, only the organizing scheme of intentions. This is the import of Bulmer's proximity principle for analysing folk classification. It leads to puzzling about the order of things in time and space, and the sequencing of human dealings with the things. The sequences have to be set within the framework of intentions. The principle forces us to the right question for ethnoscientists: Why would anyone do that?

Bulmer's proximity principle is not in any way an extension of other approaches to natural kinds. It is completely different. The focus on norms and deviation from norms starts with the similarities recognized in our own culture, a quite proper starting place for comparison. It would be amazing indeed if any other peoples came to classify according to these same groupings, starting from whatever interests and usages they have. But if the research is fixed on the idea that the similarities and anomalies that we have picked out are natural, it is doomed in advance. The proximity principle transcends the local culture by the simple assumption that in all cultures there will be grades of closeness and of distance from everyday life, and that these grades will be reflected in the taxonomic structures that are used for organizing everyday activities.

References

Barthes, R. (1967) *Elements of Semiology*. London: Cape.

Benson, F. (1979) *Aphasia, Alexia and Agraphia*. New York: Churchill Livingstone.

Bergson, H. (1896) *Matière et memoire: essai sur la relation du corps à l'esprit* (*Matter and Memory*, authorized translation by N.M. Paul and W.S. Palmer). London: Muirhead. pp. 92–100.

Bulmer, R. (1967) 'Why the cassowary is not a bird: a problem with zoological taxonomy among the Karam of the New Guinea Highlands', *Man, N.S.*, 2(1): 5–25.

Bulmer, R. (1986) 'The unsolved problem of the birds of Leviticus', in *Working Papers in Anthropology, Archeology, Linguistics, Maori Studies*. Department of Anthropology, University of Auckland.

Chesterton, G.K. (1927) 'The Song of the Fish', in *The Secret of Father Brown*. London: Cassell. Quotation from *The Father Brown Stories*, 1951. London: Ebenezer Bayliss. pp. 509–11.

Conan Doyle, Sir Arthur (1892) 'The Boscombe Valley Mystery', in *The Adventures of Sherlock Holmes*. London: Harper & Bros. Quotation from *The Penguin Complete Sherlock Holmes*, 1981. London: Allen & Lane. p. 204.

Frazer, J. (1890) *The Golden Bough*. London: Macmillan.

Goodman, N. (1969) 'Seven strictures on similarity', in *Problems and Projects*. Indianapolis: Bobbs-Merrill.

Goodman, N. (1978) *Ways of World-Making*. Cambridge: Hackett.

Jakobson, R. (1966) *Selected Writings, II. Linguistic Types of Aphasia*. The Hague: Mouton.

James, W. (1890) *The Principles of Psychology*, vol. 1. New York: Henry Holt.

Knox, R. (1928) *Footsteps at the Lock*. London: Methuen.

Lévi-Strauss, C. (1955) 'The structural study of myth', *Journal of American Folklore*, 68(270): 428–44.

Mill, James (1869) *Analysis of the Phenomena of the Human Mind*, vol. 1, new edn.

Murphy, G.L. and Medin, D. (1985) 'The role of theories in conceptual coherence', *The Psychological Review*, 92(1): 289–316.

Quine, W.V.O. (1969) 'Natural kinds', *Ontological Relativity and Other Essays*. New York: Columbia University Press. pp. 114–38.

Sayers, Dorothy L. (1945) 'The Vindictive Story of the Footsteps that Ran', *Ellery Queen's Mystery Magazine*, 6(25): 75–87.

Tversky, A. (1977) 'Features of similarity', *Psychological Review*, pp. 327–52.

8

Prospects for Asceticism

A cultural revolution

A new category of risk has emerged, a risk of irreparable damage to the commons, in which each and every one is liable to loss if the anticipated danger to the environment is actualized. It could be the occasion for a great movement of solidarity, the common risk having the effect of war in mustering altruism and collaboration. As in wartime we routinely hear the calls to cooperate by reducing our use of energy, and routinely we hear the representatives of government and the large corporations held to blame for exposing the environment to risk and denying the dangers alleged. An anthropologist observer of such a situation would wonder why the arrows of accusation fly so uniformly in one direction. It is obvious that public demand for commodities produced by the large corporations is ultimately responsible for the depredations they make on the environment. A popular movement of renunciation would be expected: public anger now demonstrating against biotechnology would be manifest against greedy consumers, private washing machines would be vandalized, stones thrown at cars in the supermarket parking lots, mobs roused to fury against airports, tourism, and the good food guides. Though there is no denying that the vocabulary of risk is politicized, and though there is a movement of renunciation, the main criticism is not against the consumer, but against authority. Which way the arrow of accusation flies is a clue to cultural bias. This chapter applies cultural theory to the question of whether the environmental movement is likely to muster enough support to change the consumption habits of the industrial nations.

If the late Victor Turner had turned his theory of social drama (1974) to the present global scene, he would surely have pointed to the repetition of two complementary plots. One narrative plot is about bringing aid where it is needed: the actors are the poor, the themes the generosity of the rich giver and the grateful recipient. In the other narrative the actors are still the poor, but this time the little person is oppressed by the big corporation, or the little nation is attacked by the coalition of the big industrial nations, the poor are ground down by the rich, the victims are little orphan children, exploited women and the devastated environment. In this second plot, the environment becomes the symbol of a revulsion against power and riches and a withdrawal of trust in government.

Now and again through human history there have been upheavals which have reshaped institutions, not by violent attack, but by cultural withdrawal. In the confrontation, values are revised and priorities regrouped, the air thick with mutual recriminations of falsehood and conflicting assertions of certainty. Recent reports on public attitudes in the UK to bio-technology cast serious doubt on the widely held view that members of the public are more likely to approve of biotechnology if they are given more accurate scientific information about it. While the public want to be informed about releases of GMO (genetically modified organisms) many do not believe that they will be told and are sceptical of information from government and industrial sources (Martin and Tait, 1993a, b, c).

I hasten to affirm that though I speak of narrative plots,

the risks at issue are real dangers. They have to be real risks because the drama is tragic and the dilemmas intractable. In the politics of risk two goods are balanced against one another: one relies on industrial development, the other looks to a return to nature. Both sides promise good health for humanity but their prescriptions are totally opposed. The speaker for development takes the central issue to be how the non-industrialized nations can develop without endangering the environment. The moral case is that modern medicine and technologies of food and transport have reduced morbidity and lowered death rates; it would be wrong not to bestow these advantages on the undeveloped world and future generations. The speaker for nature claims that industrial technology has caused the ills which modern medicine is called in to cure; famine and disease are here already, and can be laid to the door of unjust, imperialist, industrial society; alternative medicine would be better than medicine derived from modern science. Both cases rest on mutually contradictory con-struals of the facts.

I have drawn the two sides very crudely. At the edges of the political debate a more conciliatory spirit produces more informative debates, but an irreconcilable core exists, which is barely recognized by the risk analysts. For example, a small but highly influential research literature on 'social amplification of risk' (Kasperson et al., 1989) tries to explain why risks go through social processes that amplify their dangerous potential, but excludes the voluminous literature on 'risk concealment' (which is the obverse, a process of social minimization of risk), as part of these misleading processes. Scientists can isolate their reading so as to take in only the professional risk analysts' side of the argument, if they want to miss the confrontation that is being mustered under the banner of risk. But scientists cannot afford to ignore this political conflict because, as Brian Wynne (1987) has cogently shown, their credibility suffers when they allow themselves to be used to arbitrate the political issues.

The mutual mistrust goes beyond verbal exchanges. It is exhibited in cultural choices, and specially in the preferences of the young. We are indeed witnessing a popular movement of non-consumption in our midst. Some of the expressed dread of nuclear and other advanced technology is also expressed against adulterated water, bad air, and the fate of animals and plants. The whole retailing and catering industry has had to adapt to the demand for organically grown vegetables, both from a large vegetarian consumer movement, and to meet a non-vegetarian demand for organically fed, free range poultry and livestock. In the food choices alone there is ample evidence of a quiet cultural revolution which explicitly has to do with the fears for environment degradation and dislike of industrial methods of food production.

The same goes for medicine. No one can say that the demand for official medicine has declined; it has increased, but at the same time there has been a phenomenal growth in the demand for alternative medicine. The lively focus on health is plausibly a cultural response to the political salience given to risk of illness. In spite of unemployment, the economic depression and the decline of demand in general, there is a sizable public willing to pay good money for a genre of medicine which was originally defined as alternative, but now is so established that its nomenclature is continually being revised. Either it hails from the Orient, or it is folkloristic, or if it is European it has to be pre-industrial. Whatever else, it definitely does not draw its authority from advances in Western scientific theory and technology. A parallel rejection of modern medicine is expressed in the movement for the right to die. The rejection of marriage is another form of refusal to be involved in the exactions of the system.

Make of it what you will, the cultural challenge is a rejection of benefits derived from modern industrial society. I hear it self-described as a project for escaping the tyranny of unjust, inhuman, large-scale agencies and corporations. As an anthropologist I see the debate on the environment fuelled by a protest movement.

Historic movements of non-consumption

Saluting Professor Desai as the director of the Centre for Global Governance we could do well to consider Indian history and the rejection of animal sacrifice and animal food in the distant brahmanic age of Hinduism, some time before 600 BC. We could then take in the arrival of Buddhism some time later. But those two examples of non-consumption are so long ago that the kind of social documentation we would need to apply comparisons to our case is either lost or too controversial for our purpose. Much more relevant is the movement led by Gandhi in this century. This celebrated protest against imperial dominion was a movement of non-consumption. It required its followers to reject the Manchester textiles produced from machine looms manufactured in Birmingham. It professed a strong consumers' preference for home-spun, hand-dyed garments and hand-thrown pottery, and under its influence Indian economic policy still favours labour-intensive development. That was a movement of renunciation which had honourable forebears in Indian cultural history, but for interpreting the English, French and German scenes, the example is a shade exotic. India is India, and India does have these antique precursors of vegetarian, non-violent transformative movements. It would be more helpful to find exemplars nearer home.

Certainly there have been famous cases, most of them short-lived. In the scale of global environment one or two centuries of asceticism affecting a few thousand monks hardly weighs at all. But there have been some impressively big and enduring movements: for one, Christianity itself.

Historians of early Christianity describe a wave of renunciation that swept through the Roman Empire and Eastern Europe in the third century. In that case both eating and sexuality were put under severe discipline. The relevance to our times is shown by the fact that Christianity was particularly recruiting the young, who were repelled by the irrelevance of the values of the older generation, uninterested in the property transfers that were hinged on to their marriages, weary of the mindless pursuit of wealth and power, and disgusted by what they regarded as a society 'luxuriating in sexual disorder' (so the Christians stereotyped the pagan society they eventually transformed) (Brown, 1988).

Admittedly, the comparison would be more telling if sexual discipline were a prominent feature of the Green programmes today. But do not be deceived by a discrepant detail: both the Indian and the third-century Christian cases were reformist movements, both recommending austerity, both rejecting the ideals of the good life held by the generation in control. The third-century wave of asceticism evidently had as much to do with the struggle between Christian and Pagan elements for influence and power as the movement inspired by Gandhi had to do with conflict with the British. But it was also a movement of renunciation. The Christians preached the hermit's life as the ideal; every man reaching a certain age was admonished to retreat to a solitary cell, to live in self-sufficiency on spring water, eating only roots, herbs and berries. At the same time, the hermit was expected to be hospitable to visitors, sharing with them his modest vegetarian meal. Women were counselled to free themselves of the chains of conjugal life; to live as virgins was the noblest ideal. As far as forms of abstinence go, our dissenting young do not live in an age in which property and status are transferred through marriage, so choosing sexual abstinence would cause less havoc for the present system that is being blamed than it did when the young Christians of antiquity wanted to wreck the marriage webs in which they were entrapped. According to Peter Brown, the only way they could appropriate any initiative on their own account was negatively, by not marrying, not procreating, not joining or colluding with the schemes of their elders. Something more than echoes of this is to be heard in the arguments of contemporary environmentalists, and if they dislike being called 'eco-freaks' it is nothing to the rude labels their Christian opposite numbers endured.

The three movements have a certain pattern of things in common: the third-century young Christians embracing asceticism to break the chain of procreation and succession, Gandhi's movement to end British dominion in India, and the present day movement of sympathy with the threatened environment. One thing they have in common is that all three have invoked purity and truth or justice. The Christian movement venerated purity of the body, virginity, celibacy, sexual control, and the truth of the religious doctrine. Hinduism was already committed to purity of substances, Gandhi called upon justice, including justice to their own outcastes, and the Satyagraha movement was named for firmness in truth. The contemporary environmental movement calls for purity of air, food and water, and justice for the deprived, and it condemns its opponents for falsehood, lies and concealment of risks. For all three the strategy adopted is one of withdrawal and renunciation; they all should be classed as movements of non-consumption. All three are marked by charismatic leadership and grassroots support. The two historic movements were extremely successful. They did not fade away, but left effects on the institutions of their time which endure to this day.

It is not too daring to ask whether a spontaneous movement of abstinence may not hold out hope for the problems of the environment. What are the chances that the movement will increase and snowball to major proportions? Is it a threat, or a fad? Will it peter out? To clamp down on it would be absurd. A democratic government does not clamp down on consumer choice. There are no laws against abstaining from good food. In this perspective it suddenly becomes important to study what is known about ascetic movements, where they recruit their supporters, how they keep their organization going without central direction, what the prospects are for their future growth. And some of us might want to know why we are not more deeply engaged than we are.

The chances of a great wave of asceticism engulfing the West being so remote, the study sounds frivolous. But the Greens might conceivably persuade us in the industrial democracies to go on foot or by bicycle, to wear warmer clothes, wash them less, reduce house heating, eat raw foods, abstain from meat, travel less, strive less frantically to keep ourselves alive, avoid pesticides and other noxious poisons. In other words, is it unreasonable to suppose there could be a public revulsion against present levels of energy demand, such as to make a tangible difference to the problem of global warming (Rayner, 1991)? Could domestic abstention achieve a revolution that would make global governance unnecessary? It could certainly make a great difference to the problem (Fischer-Kowalski and Haberl, 1993). It sounds a remote chance to older generations, and less so to the young.

It sounds unserious to sociologists because it raises questions that are unanswerable in sociology. But an anthropological approach can break the issues down to empirically testable propositions. Within the framework of cultural theory the probability of an effective wave of austerity is capable of being discussed, factors can be identified and comparisons made. I have another reason for choosing the subject today: it is not one on which hard scientists are ever called upon to pronounce, so they need not fear that the anthropology of risk is poaching on their preserve or subverting their definitions of reality.

Risks and global governance

When the Royal Society published the *Study Group Report on Risk Assessment* (1983) 'risk' was then already a term emerging into politics, and in the interim it has become a leading concept in political debate. To have exposed the public to risk is now one of the most effective charges of misconduct that can be flung at a statesman. Among the engineers and professional risk analysts the word 'risk' still keeps its meaning to do with probabilities, but in newspapers and in Parliament its meaning has broadened to mean causing exposure to damage and devastation (Douglas, 1990). In 1992 the Royal Society published an updated report with terms of reference that included risk perception and management.

Notice that this time the report was not published as a

report of the Society, but as a report of the study group. The Preface declares that the views expressed in the report are those of the authors alone, or of those quoted by them (1992, p. iii). This was because the two chapters covering the social scientists' work do not combine well with the chapters on risk estimation by engineers, or with those on toxicology, nutrition and epidemiology. Instead of a Report of the Royal Society, we therefore have six independent reports from the different members of the working party, offered to contribute to an ongoing debate. A joint meeting of the Foundation for Science and Technology and the Royal Society was held to introduce the study to various constituencies in risk studies. At this meeting the Chairman of the working party, Sir Frederick Warner, expressed the reservations of physical scientists faced with the ambiguities of social science formulations. In a published comment he later wrote as if he regretted having opened the hospitality of his pages to anthropology. Praising the solid work achieved by psychologists, who by careful sampling and psychometric analysis have described the social amplification of risk and identified a 'dread factor' (which sums what the public dreads), he says that 'they reckoned without the anthropologists who dismiss their contributions' (Warner, 1992). He concluded by deploring the isolation of scientists: 'It is hard to face the fact that scientists are isolated in Parliament, and have little influence in decision making compared with 50 MPs from the London School of Economics', words which made the LSE sound like a rotten borough. We shall have more to say about the dangers of isolation.

One particular term, the 'social construction of risk', seemed to cause scientists much discomfort. Evidently there is the idea that some concepts are free of social construction and can claim therefore a greater degree of reality. By choosing the processes of social construction for their field, the social scientists are taken to imply that there are no hard facts, and that risks are not real either.[1] The word 'construction' sounds like fabrication, and so artificial, fictional, subjective: yet every possible concept is a construal. There can be no such thing as an unconstrued idea. I suggest that the words 'social construal of risk' might offend fewer sensibilities. There can be private construing, but all the facts that are worth formal examination have been construed in a social process. Those processes in which judgements are formed cannot be ignored or swept under the carpet.

The topic of this chapter has been chosen to show that there is a valid field of research on risk which does not contest facts with scientists. The theme of governance provides exactly the right context, not just because of fear that political chaos threatens the global environment, or because recourse to violence is a present danger, nor even because war is the most devastating cause of environmental disaster, all good reasons for invoking the social sciences. The special merit of starting with governance is that it goes to the question of justice and legitimacy, which lies at the heart of the current public discourse on risk (Laufer, 1993).

The starting point for cultural theory is any grave matter in which the debaters are in total disagreement about the facts. Michael Thompson calls this situation one dominated by 'contradictory certainties'. Among scientists such disagreement can generally be sorted out, but when the issue involves conflicting theories of justice, the discrepant evidence has been selected on moral grounds. Then it is no good preaching and no good adducing more facts, because where justice is concerned, compromise is unacceptable and reformulation suspect.

171

The three biggest dangers to the environment are diagnosed as coming from over-population in the poor countries, from energy use in rich countries, and from large-scale development projects intended to bridge the technological gap between rich and poor. If the environmentalists call for a stop to industrial development they are reproached for countenancing an unacceptable level of poverty in the non-industrial world. In a vicious circle overpopulation threatens the environment, over-population is associated with poverty, industrialization is proposed as the solution to poverty, but industrialization further degrades the environment. Essentially the locus of the problem is the industrial nations' effective demand for wealth and energy, the resulting maldistribution and, added to this, the further injustice of refusing the non-industrialized nations the right to become equally heavy users of energy. A moderate solution would seem to be very carefully apportioned development, which implies globe-wide administrative measures to which the national governments must make commitments, and be able to honour. In this perspective ungovernability works against the prospects for a safe environment.

A country can become ungovernable for all sorts of reasons. The people may be divided on hostile ethnic lines, the government may be corrupt, tyrannical, oppressive, the institutions of representation may be ineffectual, the infrastructure of communications may have collapsed. One response is to try to control chaos by clamping down on movements of public protest. If governance implies control, then global governance would imply control on a global scale. However, a settled dislike of large systems of control is a contemporary cultural theme. It becomes manifest in what Thompson, Ellis and Wildavsky (1990) call 'system blame'. Most politicians hope that with some tinkering here and there the governmental machine will work. But when the public places responsibility for present ills not on particular politicians, particular institutions, or particular government decisions, but on the whole rotten system we have 'system blame'. When any form of government is suspect, even local government, and especially national government, it is hardly propitious to talk of global governance for solving minor, still less for major, environmental problems.

Cultural theory

Sociology has made various approaches to movements of moral dissent. Some of the approaches are psychological, but nothing can be gained from considering symptoms of the individual psyche without studying the eliciting cultural framework. Deprivation theories are a branch of psychological explanation in which the explanatory idea, deprivation, is so elastic that it fits any conceivable situation. Some students separate secular movements from religious movements and treat them as two distinct kinds of phenomena, another mistake. Equally mistaken is to study a religious movement separately from its social background. Separating political movements from culture is another weakness. Most attempts to write about culture in a political context treat values and ideas as if they exerted influence while floating free above the social situation. A distinguished exception was the 1963 analysis of the 'civic culture' by Almond and Verba (1965; see also Douglas, 1993). It came close to our theme of the citizen's perception of risk by examining the citizen's sense of competence in influencing government. Its weakness was to suppose that communication between governed and government is unproblematical. Unfortunately, setting up

173

machinery of communication is not enough to resolve contradictory certainties and fundamental disagreements about justice. Concepts of justice are constituent elements in social behaviour, not external factors. For our purpose, most theories of political culture fail in having so little to say about cultural conflict. Or if they do address cultural conflict, as do many anthropologists, they tend to say nothing about politics. The major innovation is Aaron Wildavsky's work on political culture, on which the following pages largely depend for their inspiration (Douglas and Wildavsky, 1982; Wildavsky, 1991; Wildavsky and Ellis, 1988).

The anthropological theory of culture starts from the distribution in a community of different attitudes to authority and fairness. Thus it directly addresses divergent ideas of justice and different allocations of blame. Furthermore, the theory starts from social organization. It postulates that in any community the holders of power will have a limited range of strategies for securing their positions, and dealing with criticism. Just as you cannot be in two places at once, or cannot give away your cake and eat it, you cannot indefinitely go on making contradictory promises, though many, including politicians, may try. The critics, rivals and other opponents will likewise have a limited range of strategies. It is a commonplace that the life of a community depends on a normative debate about how it should conduct its affairs (Douglas, 1989). This theory adds that the life of culture, manifesting itself in this debate, is inherently adversarial. There is nothing wrong with its tendency to polarize; blaming the adversary is how the culture defines its own logical structure.

Because it survives adversarially a culture develops a distinctive morality, and associated preferences become adopted as badges of allegiance (see Chapter 4). Choice of

174

food, clothes and music, as well as religion and politics, are packaged and thrown into the contest. As Michael Thompson and Michiel Schwarz (1989) put it, exactly the opposite of 'divided we fall', the motto for cultural survival is 'divided we stand'. Culture thrives on opposition. This is such a vital insight for the way that culture generates political debate, and so relevant to the environmental issues, that it needs emphasis. There is another well-accepted sense of 'culture', this is the sense that refers to the arts, music and literature, language, and traditions and implies nothing about conflict. Keeping that more bland and historical sense in mind, you will not be able to follow this argument, which uses culture in a technical sense developed for a theoretical purpose. In this technical sense any community, however small, has in embryo four cultural types, each in debate with the others, and each anchored in a particular relation to power and authority.

Why four types? Because in order to do the study we have to focus on stable positions, and as culture is in continual process of shifting, the theory chooses a starting point with anchorage. Each type of culture is a bid for space, time and resources for a particular form of social organization. So cultural theory finds anchorage in four possibilities of organization and any cultural controversy can be typified as a debate between four positions. One is a position of commitment to authority exercised through traditional rules; it is a whole system of organization by formal distinctions and delegations and divisions of responsibility. Call it hierarchy, unless you have a principled objection to whatever it is that you normally include under that term. Call it a complex collective if you cannot use 'hierarchy' objectively. The benefit of cultural theory is to provide distance and objectivity, so it is useful not to load a neutral model with terms of opprobrium or

175

personal loyalty. An egalitarian form of community life makes an opposing slot in the scheme. It is filled of course by that part of the community which objects to the hierarchical vision. At the family level of community life this place in the cultural spectrum is often filled by the younger members; in larger units, towns, tribes, nations, it is the place for the dissenting minorities (including religious and non-religious groups).

Hierarchy and dissenting groups are opposed to one another on the issue of structure: hierarchists restrain free negotiation for the sake of a structured whole; dissenting enclavists complain against a particular preordained structure. There are two more extreme positions to name. One is for commitment to individual negotiation (the individualist's position), and the other is where a person is unable either to negotiate individually or to join a group (the isolate's position). These are the four positions on the cultural map in Figure 2.1 (see above p. 43).

At this point attention flags. The thing sounds too complicated. On the other hand, the thing sounds too static (Bellaby, 1990), or arbitrary (Rip, 1991).[2] The scheme is not devised for asking questions about everything, but it is good for investigating the conditions under which commitment to established values flourishes. Consequently it provides a basis for considering whether the environmental movement might acquire enough authority to recruit the world to its banner.

The two dimensions of the social field are structural and group constraints. These produce the four elements of the cultural theory model. The cultures are protagonists in a debate about control. A community organized by structure with group loyalty spells hierarchy. Living in a structure which others have organized, that is, structure without group loyalty, makes for isolation. Group loyalty without structures characterizes the opponents of hierarchy, the dissenting enclaves. Minimum group and minimum structure give the social environment that favours the individualist's preference for free negotiation. Each type is in tension with the rest (see Figure 2.2, p. 45).

Casting blame is one of the quotidian tests of cultural affiliation. It follows from the adversarial nature of cultural definition that each type of culture has its distinctive pattern of blaming. Who gets blamed, and for what? Hierarchy lays blame on weak definition of responsibilities, that is on inadequate organization. Individualists blame hierarchists for blocking freedom of action and enclavists for attacking their profits. Dissenting groups are essentially organized for moral criticism, their blame tends to be cast against the whole system and the badness of people's hearts. A community tending to encourage angry 'system blame' is showing signs that its culture is moving towards the bottom right-hand corner of the diagram; cultural theory will indicate the organizational changes that have helped the shift, and also what cumulative economic and political changes the cultural change will bring about.

The tension between hierarchy and individualism receives plenty of attention in social science literature, because its polarization is overt in institutions. In the Middle Ages it was the conflict between hereditary nobles and the burghers, in the nineteenth century it was the conflict between the landed and the mercantile interest, since modern times it is known as the tension between bureaucracy and markets. It is not an accident that these two types have received formal analysis in social sciences, for they are manifest in contests for power: in cultural theory hierarchy and individualism make the positive diagonal. These two cultural types take a positive attitude to power and authority: they want it. The other two constitute the negative diagonal, which has been treated either not at all, or unsystematically: the isolates only appear as a social problem, and the dissenting enclavists are treated separately as religious sects. These separations are arbitrary, and the merit of cultural theory is to offer a model that embraces all four types.

The negative diagonal

Today I will try to make up for that neglect by focusing on the negative diagonal (that is to say the diagonal B–D in the diagram of cultural conflict in Figure 2.2). It is negative not only because it has not got power, and does not aim for power, but also one half of it, the dissenting group, is negative in the sense of its austere abstention from the good things of life as defined by the other cultures. This focus will allow us to examine the relation between the two halves of the negative diagonal. We can find reasons in cultural conflict for why the environmentalist movement does not succeed in recruiting all those who have been thrown into isolation by the workings of the industrial process. If they could count on the support of the isolates they would be powerful indeed. And cultural theory can suggest what the environmental movement would need to do to itself to be empowered to transform the world. It explains why it is difficult and unlikely to be done. It can also explain why those of us who do not respond to the call to austerity can stand aside from the great contemporary challenge.

When all is said and done, we do not know nearly enough about the different kinds of minority dissent and the kinds of cultural niches they make for themselves. There are several kinds of dissenting groups, some of which do not belong on the negative diagonal at all. The crux for cultural theory is whether they are interested in getting and holding power. To classify them in cultural theory's terms, their attitude to control, territory and wealth are decisive indicators. A dissenting group that counts these things as goals is to be located on the positive diagonal. A minority aiming to become the party in power, whatever it may say about the virtues of equality, will not eschew authority in its internal relations, and it may even be prepared to use violence to gain its ends. This test will divide the IRA and many other political activists from movements on the negative diagonal, for reasons which need to be explained.

Culture is the organization that is achieved by individual commitment. If the theory were about what can be achieved by force it would not be about culture. Though prisoners are physically coerced to stay in prison, once there, they develop a prison culture within the limits of the possible. The range of possibilities and the different effects of constraints are what cultural theory is about. Each kind of culture sets cultural constraints on its adherents, and persuades them to establish the physical coercions that sustain it. Think about hierarchy and observe how easily it endows itself with formidable powers of reward and punishment. Think about individualist market society and observe how the right to exit from the market sustains and how contract law reinforces the system. Now think about the dissident enclave and ask what sort of equivalent coercions are available for ensuring that members collaborate and accept leadership.

Many cultural coercions are possible within the sect – scorn, ridicule, exhortation – but what sort of physical coercion? The difference between the dissident minority and the other groups is that no physical constraints can be imposed to stop members from leaving. If the cult leaders or sectarian pastors were to beat their recalcitrant members, they could be reported to the outside authorities and prosecuted for assault. Or even if they were merely to threaten unruly followers, the threat will not serve to stop defection. Listing the limits of the possible, the first that sets the mood for a dissenting minority's typical culture is that it can offer no political rewards and apply no punishments of any kind.[3] Enthusiasm is its only guarantor.

This sets distinctive limits on the organization of the dissident enclave. It is always in peril of losing adherents. Its leaders must disclaim authority on their own account and be very careful what kinds of impositions they can make on the tolerance of their followers. Leakage is its main preoccupation. Characteristically the dissident group is weakly organized, leadership is lacking, and it cannot tolerate distinctions of rank. From this beginning, the dissident group has to choose its goals carefully: anything requiring long-term and specialized organization will be inherently impossible; where enthusiasm is generated, it can organize for short bursts of collaboration, but it does best to make its statements negatively, by protest.

These constraints distinguish the truly dissident group from other minorities, such as governments in exile, or groups of mafioso, or activist political groups whose goal is to recover lost territory or political rights. The dissident group, defined by its dissidence, has nothing like so much to offer its members in return for their loyalty, and this gives it the distinctive moral superiority. Everything it does is disinterested. It is not realistic to plan for its taking power. The others, however far off their political or financial goal may hover, and for however long they have to claim unrequited devotion from their followers, can promise wealth and power once the goal has been attained.

This gives possibilities of effective organization and incentives for obedience and loyalty quite outside the scope of the sectarians or other dissident groups on the negative diagonal.

Taking these criteria back to the example of third-century Christianity and the contemporary environmental movement, it would seem that the Christians were on the negative diagonal before the conversion of the emperor Constantine moved them across, and the environmentalists still are.

A group with clear territorial or political objectives will know its enemies, whoever is holding on to the disputed goods. Such a group does not seek to recruit from the world at large, its object is to assert its own members' claims against a defined opponent. This puts Gandhi's achievements apart from those of the environmentalists whose opponents are only diffusely indicated: whereas Gandhi confronted the British Raj, the enemies of the environment have no particular skin complexion, no single national provenance or religion.

It is difficult to assemble a single known enemy for the environmentalist movement, which makes their self-identity harder to achieve. And again, they themselves, the environmentalists, are not the victims, they are protesting on behalf of another victim, nature. So the environmentalists are at a disadvantage compared with political activists who can overcome the problem of weak leadership by holding out private incentives to offer their following when they accede to power, or a well-defined opponent threatening to take away what they have already. They are caught in the dilemmas of altruism which have been so well staked out by the theory of collective choice.

Then again, if survival at any cost was their goal, the nature of their concerns disadvantages them. They may not

181

close their ranks and become an exclusive sect. Exclusivity, which helps other dissident minorities to survive, is not available to environmentalists. Steve Rayner's early research among extreme Maoist groups in London (1974) showed that isolation allows a group to indulge in a private, specialized time/space continuum, and to entertain strange technological fantasies. Mercifully, the environmentalists cannot afford to be exclusionary, they exist to make converts. In this they contrast with the kind of fundamentalist religious group whose objective is to reclaim the world for the religion as taught by its founder. Many a fundamentalist group has got territorial interests, the land where the God first appeared among humans, the important shrines of its history, and some homeland territory for its worshippers (Bayly, 1993). So far from being peaceful in its activism, this kind of group may be very violent.

These points combine to suggest important limitations on the ability of the environmentalist movement to do as well in influencing events as the Christians of late antiquity or the Indians of our own times: weak leadership, no territorial claims or other incentives for their followers, no clearly defined opponent, and if it were to come to sheer survival, no way of enclosing themselves in an exclusive, high-minded community. These conditions give them a major governance problem for their internal relations. What about external relations? Do they recruit as successfully as the importance of their cause deserves?

Since each cultural type is aligned against the others, embracing one point of view, no one is free to embrace all the others. This is why it is possible to stand aside and resist joining the movement. Trade unionist leaders are going to be under pressure, if it comes to a choice, to make jobs a priority over the forests, industrialists responsible to shareholders will make profits their priority. More than sectional interests, loyalty and integrity are at issue. For everyone located on the positive diagonal, friends and supporters are breathing down the necks of possible defectors, and scanning behaviour for signs of defection. At least the isolates on the other side of the negative diagonal can be expected to be free of prior commitment. They ought to be easier to recruit. Every time their ranks receive a new influx from discards and drop-outs, the environmentalists might expect a shift of opinion towards their cause.

The cultures on the positive diagonal are always busy classifying and discarding incompetents, deviants, traitors and weaklings. Nobody on the positive diagonal cares too much what happens to the discards. But the moral dissenters have two good occasions to use them. First, victims are necessary for demonstrating the case against injustice. Complaint on behalf of victims is how the culture of dissident groups declares its identity and defines its principles against other cultures. The corner for isolates is the main source for victims. And so the plight of widows and orphans, and that of the masses of poor and the refugees, enable the dissenting groups to make their case. Secondly, the dissenters woo the isolates with the hope of enrolling them among the critics of the establishment. But though the isolates afford the natural field of recruitment for a deserving movement, the corner for moral protest is already crowded with recruiting sects and enclaves. The courtship is competitive and not so easy as one might expect.

Isolates

Like all the other positions on the diagram, being an isolate is a matter of degree. The test of being an isolate is restriction of choice. The only freedom of action that a person has after paying social dues is personal. Thoughts are free, intimate behaviour is free, but for everything else a price in collaboration is exacted and anyone who is paying that price is not an isolate. The real inhabitants of this corner, who are not involved in collaboration, are some of the poor, some beggars and tramps and some persons occupying very highly esteemed positions. The position of queen and membership of the royal family are so heavily fenced with rules that the incumbent person has virtually no options, and so they may qualify as isolates. Some well-paid professions allow their superstars no scope for judgement whatever, for example, champion weight-lifters. Some choose this cultural niche for personal prefer-ence, and live there happily, with or without a sufficiency of means. Though others may see their presence as proof of victimage, it is not obvious that the inhabitants of the isolates' quadrant are all there unwillingly.

Officially part of the community but marginal, isolates are of course highly constrained in what they can do. As the unpredictable element in elections, social theory tends to take notice when they suddenly come out of their corner and coalesce around some big issue. They are described as 'alienated', a delegitimating term, or the 'floating vote' in elections, or the 'don't knows' in the survey responses. They are the 'apathetic', the 'passive' or the 'fatalists' in reports on campaigns about environmental risk. They do not deserve this neglect for they are interesting in them-selves, and interesting as potentially the majority in any particular population. It behoves us to look more closely at the negative diagonal, for along it the tension between the dissenting groups and the isolates must be central to questions about governability.

Any great dislocation of institutions could send vast numbers to inhabit here. The isolates' corner would fill up as a result of changes such as deskilling the workforce. Economic depression could cause an increase in the number of the rejected and increase the ranks of permanently unemployed. If casualization of labour were to increase, and temporary staff came to outnumber permanent employees in the population (Morrow, 1993), a higher proportion of the community would be located in that cultural niche. According to *Time Magazine* in March 1993, temporary employment had increased since 1982 by 250 per cent. What are called 'contingent workers' are expected by the year 2000 to be half of the workforce of the United States. The industrial process that is reducing mutual involvement and responsibility is channelling a larger proportion of the community to the isolate's quadrant. Such a transformation of the community would produce a stronger bias to the negative diagonal, both to apathy and to dissent. Waves of immigration might have the same effect as casualization, but not necessarily. Much depends on the prior organization and cultural bias of the immigrants and their hosts.

We have named some of the disadvantages that beset environmentalists in comparison with religious sects and contestants for political power. In attracting new members they all face another barrier: isolates tend to become confirmed in their cultural bias.

The isolates' cultural barrier

I do not wish to reinforce the contempt those on the positive diagonal feel for the isolates. Sir Frederick Warner, cherishing a misapprehension that religion makes for fatalism, remarks that 'natural disasters are accepted by the overwhelming number of fatalists in the world who believe in re-incarnation, the reception into the bosom of Allah, or in an after-life in a Heaven of variously perceived delights'

(1992, p. 47). Such a lumping together of all manner of alien beliefs is what cultural theory is designed to correct. Remember that the best conditions for original thought were once held to be isolation, for Edward Gibbon said that isolation was the price of insight, 'Conversation enriches the understanding, but solitude is the school of genius' (quoted by Shapin, 1990). When we presume to characterize a culture of the isolates, it has to be in respect of the way that the society in which they have so little part affects them, and their ruses for escaping its control.

An isolate thinks idiosyncratically, the more isolated the more eccentric the train of ideas. Since isolates achieve so little coordination with other people how can they have a typical culture? I argue that without forming a community they march in step, so their culture can have an external coherence when viewed from outside. Their irregular and inconsequential connection with the rest of society gives them a common holding. For example, just because they are not under pressure to synchronize their arrivals and departures, the isolates tend to keep peculiar hours and cherish private notions of time.[4] Their activities being decoupled from coordination with others, they acquire a common experience of deadlines overstepped and appointments missed. In common they see disapproval or amusement in the faces of others more tightly keyed into social life, and a common self-image develops. Without knowing that the others are doing the same, isolates justify their own vagaries by self-deprecatory joking, or they plead a feckless disposition to mollify frustrated friends, creditors or agents of the law.

The isolates' distinctive cultural style is not a matter of psychological predisposition. Their far-out eclecticism has become a protective barrier against pressure. Uncommitted to persuading anyone to do anything, they are not trying to persuade or organize. If they once did such things, they have learnt the uselessness of it in their present position. Along with being accommodated to isolation comes relief that no one expects very much from them. Another experience which they all may have, though it would be going too far to call it a shared experience, is the sense of pressure lifted. There is less scope for disappointment. As to hopes, a dose of fatalism is a good adaptation: then there will be no bad surprises. It is not surprising that the long-term inhabitants of the isolates' corner have in common a tendency to apathy.

As to intellectual bias, they can give rein to fancy. No one minds if they contradict themselves or leave their arguments unfinished; no one is listening. Whatever their educational background, they share an interest in the occult. A single issue of the American journal the *National Enquirer* (3 May 1988) ran several articles on miracle healing and instant overcoming of pain; transcending the separation of death, by ghosts, curses, and finding out who your lovers were in past lives; advertisements for palmistry, magic for winning large sums of money, or losing weight, or winning in love; and two articles on the reality of extra-terrestrial beings (after 30 years of government and military cover-up). This undiscriminating occultism is a far cry from the organized beliefs in an after-life which attracted Sir Frederick's derision. True isolates live in a state of eclectic openness where anything might be expected to happen. Their main freedom is one that other people fight for: freedom to believe what they like, whenever they like.

Conclusions for cultural theory

Risk analysts have developed a whole field called 'risk communication'.[5] If its experts would recognize that each

187

cultural sector only hears its own kind of communication they would surely be calling for cultural audits. Information simply does not rub off on someone who is never going to make use of it. Happy with their undemanding lot, isolates tend to construe the universe benignly. They will not take bad news about global warming more seriously than imminently expected attacks by ghosts and vampires. It would be better for the prospects of a serious environmental debate that less of the population should be living under this banner. Rather than trying to communicate a complex idea to people who are not interested, it would be better to prevent a large population from being driven against their wishes into the role of uninvolved isolate.

At the end of the argument, the outlook for understanding the processes by which risks are construed is more cheerful. At least there is a way of communicating with each other about cultural bias. It will become easier to substantiate the claims of the theory as survey data accumulates. The Report of the Royal Society's Working Group correctly observed that cultural theory was short on empirical support (1992, p. 113) but that is in the process of being remedied. Karl Dake and his colleagues are successfully characterizing the public according to cultural bias and relating attitudes to risk to political and cultural affiliation (Dake, 1992). There is now a viable and more comprehensive alternative to psychological theories of risk aversion.

On the other hand, our conclusion is gloomy for the prospect that a new wave of austerity might save the environment by reducing the demand for energy. It is much harder to make eco-conversions than some may have thought, and harder for a movement on the negative diagonal to make itself effective. Attitudes to authority are part of the limiting conditions for each kind of culture. For example, if environmentalists were to be very effective in organizing beyond protest demonstrations or propaganda, they would need to institute internal authority. But this would be incompatible with a position on the negative diagonal. For any group organized as a protesting minority, the problem of stemming defection will tend to overwhelm their agenda. Someone would have to play Emperor Constantine to their role of Christians renouncing the world's pomps, so that they could enjoy the strengths, incentives and credibility of the positive diagonal. And the imperial role is in heavy disrepute just now.

On the cheerful side, again, cultural theory makes it easier not to be bogged down in arguments which revolve around contradictory certainties. It would be better for the cause of the environment for it not to be used as a ploy in a debate about legitimation. Identifying the real issue as cultural conflict, the new kind of dialogue about the environment would squarely face the issue of justice. Instead of bandying blame, the new dialogue would concentrate on the kind of society that would be compatible with an environment under continual scrutiny and control. Making the stark choices visible would be a considerable progress.

It would also be progress to recognize that apathy, indifference and intellectual non-commitment are in themselves forms of cultural commitment, and are part of a package. If there is reason to think that the industrial system is sending too many of us into the fold of apathetics and indifferents, research should be done to audit our cultural commitment. The environmentalists need to know how much of the population at any one time gets cast into the corner for isolates, and how many isolates are moving out to join the other dissenting groups, which ones are

189

attracted by the positive and which by the negative protest. The relative strength of the four corners is theoretically able to be estimated because the cultural audit depends on features of the economy and institutional life of the community.

Notes

1 This is a surprisingly common misunderstanding of the position in cultural theory, sometimes surprisingly naive, as in a book which has philosophical pretensions written into its title: S.K. Shrader-Frechette, *Risk, Rationality, Philosophical Foundations for Populist Reforms* (Berkeley, CA: California University Press, 1991).

2 The latter author (Rip, 1991, ch. 13, n. 1) is kind enough to say that the discussion of socio-cultural aspects of risk perception has been dominated by the typology of risk attitudes and behaviour drawn from cultural theory.

3 Apart from their criticism of the structures of the existing hierarchy, there are organizational reasons for why dissenting enclaves find it inappropriate and even difficult to develop their own hierarchy. See Douglas, 1987 and also Thompson et al., 1990, pp. 200–9.

4 As revealed by Gerald Mars's unpublished research on cultural bias shown in time-keeping habits in London households, discussed in Chapter 4.

5 In this regard, see Nick Pidgeon's chapter in the Royal Society report (Royal Society, 1992, ch. 5, pp. 118–23) and the long bibliography.

References

Almond, G. and Verba, S. (1965) *The Civic Culture, Political Attitudes and Democracy in Five Nations*. Princeton, NJ: Princeton University Press.

Arie, R. (1991) 'The danger culture of industrial society', in R.E. Kasperson and P.J.M. Stallen (eds), *Communicating Health and Safety Risks to the Public*. Dordrecht: Kluwer.

Bayly, Susan (1993) 'History and the fundamentalists: India after the Ayodhya Crisis', *Bulletin of the American Academy of Arts and Sciences*, XLVI (April): 7–26.

Bellaby, P. (1990) 'To risk or not to risk? Uses and limitations of Mary

Douglas on risk-acceptability for understanding health and safety at work and road accidents', *The Sociological Review*, 38(3): 465–83.

Brown, P. (1988) *The Body and Society: Men, Women and Sexual Renunciation in Early Christianity*. New York: Columbia University Press.

Dake, K. (1992) 'Characterizing the public: myths of nature: culture and the social construction of risk', *Journal of Social Issues*, 48(4): 21–39.

Douglas, Mary (1987) *How Institutions Think*. New York: Syracuse University Press.

Douglas, Mary (1989) 'Culture and collective action', in M. Freilich (ed.), *The Relevance of Culture*. New York: Bergin and Garvey. Reprinted in *Risk and Blame: Essays in Cultural Theory*. London: Routledge, 1993.

Douglas, Mary (1990) 'Risk as a forensic resource', *Daedalus, Risk*, 19(4): 1–16.

Douglas, Mary (1993) 'A quelles conditions un ascetisme environmentaliste peut-il reussir?', *La Nature en politique, ou l'enjeu philosophique de l'ecologie*. Paris: Association Descartes/l'Harmattan. pp. 96–121.

Douglas, Mary and Wildavsky, A. (1982) *Risk and Culture*. Berkeley, CA: California University Press.

Fischer-Kowalski, M. and Haberl, H. (1993) 'Metabolism and colonisation, modes of production and the physical exchange between societies and nature', *Innovation in Social Research*, 3.

Kasperson, R.E., Renn, O., Brown, S., Slovic, P., Emel, J., Goble, R., Kasperson, J.X. and Ratick, S. (1989) 'The social amplification of risk: a conceptual framework'. Reprint No. 60, Center for Technology, Environment and Development, Clark University, Worcester, MA; reprinted in *Risk Analysis*, 8: 177–87.

Laufer, R. (1993) *L'Entreprise face aux risques majeures, a propos de l'incertitude des normes sociales*. Paris: l'Harmattan.

Martin, S. and Tait, J. (1993a) *Biotechnology: Cognitive Structures of Public Groups*. Milton Keynes: Centre for Technology Strategy, Faculty of Technology, Open University.

Martin, S. and Tait, J. (1993b) *Release of Genetically Modified Organisms (GMOs): Public Attitudes and Understanding*. Milton Keynes: Centre for Technology Strategy, Faculty of Technology, Open University.

Martin, S. and Tait, J. (1993c) *Release of Genetically Modified Organisms: Public Attitudes and Understanding, Summary Report*. Milton Keynes: Centre for Technology Strategy, Faculty of Technology, Open University.

Morrow, L. (1993) 'The temping of America', *Time Magazine*, March: 40–3.

Rayner, S. (1974) 'The perception of time and space in egalitarian sects: a millenarian cosmology', in Mary Douglas (ed.), *Essays in the Sociology of Perception*. London: Routledge & Kegan Paul. pp. 247–74.

Rayner, S. (1991) 'The greenhouse effect in the US: the legacy of energy abundance', in *Energy Policies and the Greenhouse Effect*: vol. 2 *Country Studies and Technical Options*. Dartmouth: Royal Institute of International Affairs. pp. 235–77.

Rip, A. (1991) 'The danger culture of industrial society', in R.E. Kasperson and P.J.M. Stallen (eds), *Communicating Health and Safety Risks to the Public*. Dordrecht: Kluwer.

Royal Society (1983) *Study Group Report on Risk Assessment*. London: Royal Society.

Royal Society (1992) *Risk, Analysis, Perception, Management: Report of a Royal Society Study Group*. London: The Royal Society.

Shapin, S. (1990) quotation from Edward Gibbon, *The History of the Decline and Fall of the Roman Empire* (2nd edn, 1901), in 'The mind is its own place: science and solitude in seventeenth century England', *Science in Context*, 4(1): 191–218.

Thompson, M., Ellis, R. and Wildavsky, A. (1990) *Cultural Theory*. Boulder, CO: Westview Press. pp. 59–60.

Thompson, M. and Schwarz, M. (1989) *Divided We Stand: Redefining Politics, Technology and Social Choice*. Brighton: Harvester-Wheatsheaf.

Turner, V.W. (1974) *Dramas, Fields and Metaphors: Symbolic Action in Human Society*. Ithaca, NY: Cornell University Press.

Warner, F. (1992) 'Calculated risks', *Science and Public Affairs*, Winter, 44–9.

Wildavsky, A. (1991) *The Rise of Radical Egalitarianism*. Washington, DC: American University Press.

Wildavsky, A. and Ellis, R. (1988) *Dilemmas of Presidential Leadership, from Washington through Lincoln*. New Brunswick, NJ: Transaction Books.

Wynne, B. (1987) *Risk Management and Hazardous Waste: Implementation and the Dialectics of Credibility*. International Institute for Applied Systems Analysis/Springer-Verlag.

9

The Cosmic Joke

Holy joy

According to the non-believer, religion is a solemn affair, awe-inspiring, frightening even, but not a joking matter. However, the Bible prophets expound the oldest and best joke in the world, they promise that the mighty will be brought down and the lowly raised up. It is all very well for the prophets to keep telling God's great cosmic joke, they are the prophets and they can say wild things; we certainly do not look to find it extolled in the priestly work. Why not? I will argue that we have a double bias, one against the priests so that we do not expect their message to be one with that of the prophets, and another against the joke itself. After all, we who have the privilege of an academic life might well find it cuts too close to the bone. Relatively speaking, we are the mighty and to some extent the joke will be against us. It is not funny to say that the despised will receive the honours and our own works will be brought to nothing. We do not like the joke, we do not see it, and when we admiringly describe Judaism we make out it is a solemn affair with no joy and laughter.

If I try to explain how the anthropologists work, and claim that their results are not a threat to belief, in return perhaps believers will be able to tell me something about religion that the outside professionals cannot explain. What is it about religion that makes a person ready to die for it?

People seem ready to kill each other for quite trivial reasons, so why they kill for religion is not very mysterious. But why do they die for it? I suggest it is something to do with rejoicing. The inexplicable, irreducible thing that mystifies outsiders is that the Jews rejoice in the law.

It is naturally annoying for believers to find the professionals endlessly prepared to reduce religion to something else. (I am referring to anthropology, sociology, Freudian styles of psychoanalysis and philosophy.) However, when believers feel irked in this way, they can remember that there is this thing about religion that escapes reductionist analysis.

In truth, I must admit that scepticism suits the anthropologist. We write professionally about other people's religions, and it would be unreasonable to expect us to believe in them all. We study taboo, symbolism, blessing and curses; oracles and magic come into our purview. But largely our effort is to make sense of what we find. We are not there to pour contempt or to despise. If an anthropologist can only attribute nonsense to a ritual or a text, it is a confession of defeat. In spite of our coming out of a strong sceptical tradition there is nothing specifically atheist about the anthropologists' part in it. You will meet the occasional old-fashioned anthropologist who takes all religion for mumbo-jumbo. The professional attitude is undenominational. Scepticism becomes the anthropologist simply because of the huge variety of religions in the world. But for the devout believer the anthropologist's striving after objectivity is not threatening. I will try out an anthropological interpretation of the *kashrut*, the forbidden animal foods, to illustrate that anthropology can even be a support to belief. The Jews when they gather together will celebrate with good food, but they will not eat shrimps, squid, crab or prawns, or ham. I am not going to talk about all their food rules, but only about the rejection of the particular animal species decreed in Leviticus.

Many different reasons are given for the rules, but the reasons do not usually come out of Leviticus itself. For example, an old tradition teaches that the pig is forbidden because it is a scavenger. But the book says nothing whatever about scavenging, and the scavenging explanation does not help to explain the forbidding of the camel, the hare and the rock badger. Scavenging does not explain why water creatures without fins and scales cannot be eaten.

In the traditions each forbidden animal tends to get its own reason, and never one from the book. Creepy-crawly creatures, for example, are forbidden. In the book it just says that if they creep or go on their bellies they are an abomination. But the rule is taken to be based on a universal disgust and fear of snakes. This is the least convincing of all to the anthropologist, because it is not true that snakes are universally repulsive. We find it hard to name any universal feelings of disgust at all. Many people love to eat eels and snakes and esteem insects and grubs as gastronomic delicacies. Then there is the problem of the text. Are we supposed to forget that God made the creatures that crawl, and that in Genesis it says that when he had made them he found that they were good? So why are the creeping crawling creatures picked out as abominations? Again, on critical literary grounds, if the rest of the book were a muddle, we might be tempted to look for separate ad hoc explanations of each item forbidden, but in every other respect Leviticus shows logical order in a high degree. It is very systematic and not at all haphazard.

Something has gone wrong with interpreting Leviticus and I am going to blame the problems on long-standing, anti-priestly prejudice. James Frazer followed the intellectuals of his own day and considered that priestcraft is a more primitive institution than state religion, and both more primitive than science. Primitive for him meant magical, and so largely beyond rational interpretation. In the same mood we have fallen easily into the idea that the priestly part of the Pentateuch is so antique as to be primitive and so need not be expected to make sense in its own terms. It is not good enough in modern anthropology to interpret the priestly books of the Bible in terms of what we know about deep psychological aversions, or what we know about other religions of the region at the time in terms of what archaeology can dig up, but not in terms of what can be dug out of the book itself, assuming it to be an intellectually coherent composition.

God through a prism

The anthropologist's question to the believer is why it could be disturbing to learn that almost every people have got their own description of God. With each their own account of creation, their own history of divine intervention, their own ideas of what counts as sin, God is split into a myriad refractions through the prism of religious doctrines. Trying to organize the motley stuff, the anthropologist finds some religions are polytheist, some monotheist, some ritualist, some ecstatic. Some concentrate on healing the body, others specialize in penitence. The sheer variety calls irresistibly for explanation, but why is that worrying?

In Northwestern University I had the privilege of teaching an introductory course in the Department of History and Literature of Religions. After the first few weeks a student dropped my course saying that it was causing him to lose his faith. The head of department sent for me and I was nervous (because Edmund Perry is a devout Methodist). But he jovially declared that anyone would be better off without a faith which was so easily shaken. Indeed, if a believer does not know that the idea of God is battered about by believers, their faith is sheltered indeed. In my opinion, inquiry into the background of faith must be a good thing, like meditation on the Law. Why should anyone's faith be under attack from discovering that someone else does not share it? Is my faith fixed in childhood? Does faith impose a censorship on what I can learn about other people? If so, it is a sad outlook for anthropology.

The sceptical tradition of anthropology has long roots. We are offspring of the Enlightenment. I refer you to the Encyclopedia Britannica of 1773, first edition, article on Mythology. There you learn that there are three kinds of religion. First, idolatry, full of popular magical superstitions; second, priestly religion, deceiving the people in the interest of kings; then the philosophy of religion, which seeks earnestly to know about God, beauty and truth. Note that this triple division separates what the anthropologist in the field finds to be one single experience. Magic for personal health and private love is separated from rituals for the seasonal calendar, philosophy to explain it all is separated again.

The sceptical tradition thrives on making divisions between parts of religion, picking out one part to be admired and one to be rejected, one to be a strength and the other to be a weakness of human nature. This very dividing makes a mesh through which the regular experience of religious people slips away unnoticed. When James Frazer separated magic from priestcraft, and priests from divine kings, he was closely following the separations of the eighteenth-century Encyclopedists. He also dismissed the whole superstitious caboodle of religious practice as fossil relics, left-over traces of the evolution of mind. The only thing in religion that is of value after magic has been superseded by science, and sacred kingship by constitutional monarchy, in his opinion is poetry. The rest could be ignored; the enduring strand was the old-age meditation on existence arising from our poetic imagination.

In modern times the philosophers and psychologists have continued to exalt the imagination and downgrade constraints upon it. You recognize the two columns into which secular judgement pours religious behaviour: imagination is separated from reason and law; spontaneity and informality are preferred over formality; human feelings of compassion and righteous anger are justified while calculated reason is regarded as mercenary, cold, mechanical. A strong popular bias downgrades one column, the religion of ritual, and upgrades the other, charismatic religion. I will be arguing that often the same religion offers both opportunities of worship, and that this is true of the Bible.

If anyone believes that their own faith is strong enough to resist secular culture, let them test how well they resist current secular bias as they read the Bible. The non-religious world encourages us to choose between these two columns, priestly and controlled versus prophetic and spontaneous. It is hard to resist letting your choice fall against public rituals and in favour spontaneous private worship. Consider for example your attitude to the priesthood. In the secular tradition anti-clericalism is so strong that it is almost impossible to imagine the good priest, the beloved shepherd of his flock, guardian of the people. Judaism has always had its own anti-clericalism, but now it is added to the strong secular trend. Reflecting this bias, I observe that the priestly editors of the Bible are nowhere nearly so popular as the prophets and psalmists, and even the kings.

As an anthropologist I feel relatively immune. Our

training is to observe dispassionately, not to judge. In our records are all these kinds of religion, ritualist as well as ecstatic, and many kinds of prophets and many kinds of priests (but they are called diviners, officiants, shrine guardians). With this training and this immense variety it is easier to resist secular bias, though we respond to bias of another kind: the joke has it that each anthropologist becomes enamoured of his tribe. We tend to divide religion into ritual, mythology, symbolism, sacrifice, witchcraft, divination and so on. We also tend to specialize among these topics, so sometimes there is little conversation to be had if one colleague has had a lifetime of work on symbolism and another colleague has spent a lifetime on sacrifice. But I think I can say that the professional anthropologists' splitting up of religion carries remarkably little prejudice from secular life and European history. So far from being anticlerical they defend the local priests against the missionaries. You may even hear them declare that some of their best friends are priests.

Religious physics

Admittedly anthropologists take a sceptical attitude to the religion they are studying. If pressed to use these denominational terms, they would have to say in all honesty that the claims of the religion are 'false' in respect of certain issues in what I would call 'religious physics'. There is an insurmountable conflict between religious belief and the laws of gravity, time and space. It is hard for an anthropologist to believe in levitation every time there is news of a saint who can rise up and stay in the air. It is equally hard to believe in bi-location, the power to defy space and time and be in two places at once; hard to accept that a person can be present in purely spiritual form, invisible and taking up no space at all. There is no such problem about believing in spectacular powers of healing and control of the body, and not hard to believe in extra-sensory perception, even prophecy. The major stumbling block arises from our commitment to certain fundamental laws of Newtonian physics.

You could say that the principal rift between the anthropologist and the believer is 'ontological': the theory of existence. The anthropologist who really admires the religion being studied, and who has no personal religious prejudice against it, needs to put a special bracket around the non-Newtonian physics it rests upon. Spiritual beings are so-called just because they are non-corporeal, and so enjoy the powers of ubiquity, invisibility and knowledge of what will happen at a later time. They can also confer these powers on their adepts. This dimension has to be accepted by the anthropologist if there is going to be any under-standing of explanations, excuses and accusations.

Anthropologists are not happy about using the word 'supernatural' to describe religious beliefs which defy the way we see the laws of nature. For one thing, we should not use a vocabulary which assumes that ghosts and angels are not natural. For another, we do not want to distort the religion by importing scholastic terminology from our own history. Trance and divination may be common, they may be special talents, we need to know the local theory so as to follow the thread of actions which these beliefs entail. The anthropologist's vocation is to achieve 'ethnography', that is, a precise and correct des-cription. Above all, the social anthropologist is not tempted to split the religion into non-communicating compart-ments. The same families are producing food, blaming and praising one another and sending their children to be initiated. The same people are rearing their priests and prophets, and so we expect the religion to have some underlying unity.

In this flattering light, the anthropologist would seem to offer no threat to the believer. How could there be conflict? Striving for the highest possible degree of objectivity, the anthropologist's ideal posture is respectful attention. Yet the believer can feel threatened. The threat is not from knowing about the sheer variety of religions. That is easy to deal with because the believer can say why the others are mostly wrong. The threat is from hearing them explained. When specialists try to explain religion, their theories are in terms of controls and constraints. Although Western philosophy can proudly say that it is the law that makes us free, the context is generally secular. In a strong secular tradition in the West the laws of religion are exempted from the good words said in favour of law in general; sceptics and atheists take the laws of religion to be specially restricting and not something to rejoice about. So the professionals find it convenient to overlook the fact that the Jews rejoice in the laws of their religion.

It sounds as if the anthropologist is bound to miss the point and bound to be a trouble to the believer. Indeed, in Islam such inquiry is often forbidden on the grounds that it is not for us to consider how God's revelation was made or how his plans work out. Not for us to understand the political or economic situation in which the message was first delivered. Not for us to explain God's choice of a particular moment, or a particular people. God's interventions in history are beyond speculation. No benefit can come from the pathetic human scrutiny and the very enterprise is sinful.

Of course such piety eliminates the anthropology of religion. Essentially the pious objection is to the historicizing of revelation. A message that is for all people at all times is ahistorical. How can it matter how it was produced or when? The creator's acts cannot be put under the same sort of inspection as human decisions. The basic objection of piety to anthropology is that history must not intrude into eternity; religious physics needs to be protected from threat. This is just where, with deep respect and some piety, the plea for anthropology must be made. If geographic factors are given their due in shaping a faith, then why not historical factors? If it is acceptable to examine the meanings of the desert and the wilderness in Judaism, then surely the meanings of kings and sceptres, palaces and censuses can be studied by the devout. If history is allowed, what is wrong with the anthropologist putting the Bible in the context of other religions? The special bias of anthropology is its bias against prejudice. If history and geography have influenced believers' interpretation of the Bible, anthropology may even have a role in detecting the bias.

Priests versus prophets

Following the grand secular bias against formality and ritual, in favour of feeling and spontaneity, the prophets' better reputation is understandable. Bias built into the intellectual history of the West would be enough to account for it. When we come to read the prophets, first we read of the love God has for his people, likened intimately to human love. Israel is presented as the betrothed, the bride who has been unfaithful, and who is roundly cursed by her jealous husband, but, amazingly, the Lord, whom she has rejected in running after lovers, does not reject her. In the Prophets God is altogether angry with Israel's enemies, and altogether loving and forgiving to Israel if only she will repent (Isaiah 54: 57, Hosea 2: 14). The question is whether Isaiah, Hosea, Amos and Ezekiel are teaching a different theology from that in the law books, Leviticus and Numbers.

If the prophets emphasize justice and mercy, and Leviticus emphasizes due performance of ritual, they would seem to be opposed. Do the priests who edited Leviticus give a different message from the prophets? Let us make the test the reading of Isaiah 1: 10ff. If there is a text that demeans the formal cult, it must be here. Inveighing against a sinful nation the prophet reports that the Lord wants no more burnt offerings. Is not this a direct attack on the demand for burnt offerings made in Numbers and Leviticus?

I delight not in the blood of bullocks, lambs and goats. (1: 11)

Bring no more vain oblations; incense is an abomination to me, the new moons, the sabbaths, the calling of assemblies, I cannot bear; it is iniquity. (1: 13–14)

This reads as a violent rejection of everything that the Lord told Moses in Leviticus and Numbers (Numbers 28–29).

How does Isaiah go on? Perhaps the rejection of external religion will be softened in the next verses. But no, the prophet tells the people that their hands are full of blood and to cease from doing evil (1: 15–16). He does not stop after naming iniquity and unrighteousness in general terms, but goes on to tell us about the sufferings of the victims.

He says:

Seek justice,
relieve the oppressed,
defend the fatherless,
plead for the widow.

He describes them toiling under their burdens, the plight of orphans with no father, the hardships of widows. We can almost see the poor trailing their rags, limping beggars, humble crowding in public places. In a sharp rebuke the Lord says later:

> For I the Lord, love justice. I hate robbery for burnt offering. (Isaiah 61: 8)

And it is not just an attack on sacrifice: the same attack is repeated for fasting. The prophet compares physical fasting while still committing injustice with true fasting, which requires the worshipper first to 'loosen the bands of wickedness, undo the heavy burdens, let the oppressed go free' (Isaiah 58: 7ff). And again, he contrasts empty formality with keeping the Sabbath in righteousness (Isaiah 58: 13). This is a prophet who says that the Lord wants 'a humble and contrite heart' (Isaiah 57: 15 and 66: 2).

Do these texts signal a rift between prophets and the priests? Was Isaiah's vision of Judaism a religion of the inner person, without rituals of sacrifice, a religion of righteousness and justice? If so, what happened? The priests wrote a very different-seeming law, insisting strictly on the outward forms. Our own anti-clerical traditions give a sneaking enjoyment from seeing the priests put down by the prophets. Could the priests even be the very leaders of Israel whom Isaiah berated for despoiling the poor (Isaiah 3: 12–15). If the priests were so much in the wrong, what do we feel about the observance of the Sabbath and the food laws that Leviticus was so emphatic about?

One serious look at Leviticus shows that there is no line-up of priest and prophet, and no conflict between internal versus external religion, or justice versus ritual. As I read it, Leviticus makes a truly brilliant synthesis of two equations: justice of people to people, and justice of people to God. In Leviticus the Lord tells Moses that his people are emphatically required not to oppress one another. When it describes sin, Leviticus does not focus exclusively on sins of unclean eating or contact with defiling things. Sin is lying, defrauding and robbing a neighbour (Leviticus 6: 27). Righteousness, justice and mercy, fair dealing between the people are the subject of chapter 19, and chapter 26 repeats God's demand for fair dealing and honesty, from the people to himself. Indeed, fairness and care for the poor turn out to be pre-eminent themes to which the structure of the book draws elaborate attention.

The forbidden animals

So what about the forbidden animals? What has their uncleanness got to do with justice? There is an old tradition that the animals which the people of Israel may eat and those they may not eat are allegories of virtues and vices. But which virtues and which vices? The clue to the interpretation has been missing. It may be convincing to say that the flocks and herds can be eaten because parting the hoof is a sign of choosing between the holy and the unclean, and cud-chewing a sign of meditation. But if this indicates the virtues, it does not help to identify the vices which the prohibited animals represent. What about the rules that exclude sea foods like squid, mackerel and eels because they have no scales? What is wrong with having no scales? Why should shrimp and lobster be excluded because they have scales but no fins? What do fins signify? And all the other rules? Why are locusts that crawl forbidden, those that hop allowed?

Leviticus in the chapter that contains the list gives no reason; it simply states that they are unclean and 'abominable'. There was a respected reading which gave up trying to make sense of the dietary laws and just treated them as an ancient and peculiar block sticking out from past times, like a verbal fossil, inserted in Leviticus and in

Deuteronomy out of respect for the past. This is an objectionable interpretation; it demeans the editors of Leviticus. Why ever would they have put something into the sacred book of laws which they did not understand? It is parcel with other interpretations which treat the editors as antiquarians, reverently collecting curious old laws and binding them together without too much care for coherence and sense.

Read chapter 11 carefully again. I invite you to become a temporary anthropologist; you must then expect that if a chapter is there it fits in with the rest of the book. You find that the chapter gives three habitats: earth, water, air, and in each of these there are clean animals and unclean. If we go back to Genesis we find a law which covers all the land and air animals. At creation each of the denizens of air, earth and water were expected to subsist on leaves, berries and seeds. There was going to be a vegetarian world. After the people had proved their wicked natures, in the new Covenant after the flood, God softened his law so that people could eat meat, but never blood. Meat-eating without blood-eating would be covered by a practice of draining the blood from the flesh.

But what about animals that have eaten blood? Carnivorous animals would have the blood of their victims in their flesh. The rule that restricted the people to eating herbivorous animals would take care of that. The simple rule to choose for the table only animals that divide the hoof and chew the cud automatically excludes all carnivorous and carrion feeders. So far, so good. But there are a few dubious cases: the camel though it seems to chew the cud, also the rock badger and the hare, do not part the hoof. So they are separately listed. Then the pig has neatly parted hoofs, but does not chew the cud. So the pig is listed too. But what about blood eating birds? No separate rule is given for the birds of the air: they are listed by name. Unfortunately we do not know which birds they were. But I could be happy to follow the Mishnaic tradition, which teaches that they are forbidden because they are carnivorous birds which seize their prey with their claws and tear it with their beaks.

So now we have accounted for the air and land animals on the basis of what is said in Leviticus and Genesis about not eating blood. But then there remains the rest of creation. We are left with the rules forbidding fish without fins and scales, and creeping things that go on their bellies. Think again about this class: why do they crawl? On analogy with the rest, their bodies are wrong in some way. Either they have no legs at all, like snakes and worms, or they have too many legs, too little to lift their bodies off the ground, so they crawl, like insects for example. Their extra limbs or missing parts are the only things about them that are mentioned.

Leviticus is a highly logical book. It is implausible that the priests did not have a very clear idea of what the creepy-crawlers of animal creation stood for, and unlikely that they did not explain it to the reader. They were teachers and these animals are pointed out for a teaching purpose. As we read on, we discover that Leviticus does in fact tell us a lot more about the animals and that it does make a lot of sense in the terms of their teaching about God.

After the dietary laws the next five chapters take up the theme of bodily impurity, this time applied to the people, not to animals. We realize that Leviticus is using the body for a grand analogy. First, the food laws were about what goes inside bodies, and secondly, in chapters 12–15, the laws are about what goes out of bodies. These chapters are about leprosy and all kinds of sickness that attack the skin covering of the body. All the while, we are not told what is impure or unholy about these bodily defects. We have been told clearly that no sacrificial animal can be offered if it is blemished (chapters 1–4), but again, the clue as to what blemish means is not given until later.

This is a book which reveals its meaning as it goes on. It has a riddling technique of piling one mysterious analogy on another. Not until we get to chapter 21 does it tell us what blemish is. There it says that a priest whose body is blemished may not approach the altar, and it defines blemish as a mutilation. The priest counts as blemished if he cannot see, or cannot walk, or has a limb too long or an injured foot, or is a hunchback or a dwarf (21: 18–24). Still we have not been told clearly what is unholy about blemish. In the next chapter the riddle is repeated. This time it is the same theme as at the beginning: blemished animals must not be offered. The same description is given as for the priest. Blemish means blind, disabled, mutilated, 'a part too long or a part too short' (22: 26).

What is wrong with having a part too long, or a part too short? In itself, nothing, as a figure of God's cosmos, everything. In this book, the body is the cosmos. Everything in the universe shows forth the righteousness of the Lord. Animals and humans, people and priests, animals for food, and animals for the altar, their bodies are figures of righteousness. This is all explained for us clearly in chapter 24, which describes blemish as the consequence of unrighteousness:

> When a man causes a blemish in his neighbour, as he has done, so it shall be done to him: breach for breach, eye for eye, tooth for tooth. (24: 19–20)

The context is the punishment for blasphemy. The Lord's name has been defiled, Moses has consulted the Lord, and the answer has come as a general statement on the meaning of justice.

We are told that causing a blemish means doing a damage. A breach of justice takes away from the victim, leaving too little, or imposes too much of a burden. Remember Isaiah: 'Loosen the bands of wickedness, undo the heavy burdens'. The priest who is a hunchback is a figure of one with too big a load, the priest who is a dwarf figures one who has too little, cheated of his normal share. Consider again the animals that crawl on the belly, the ones with the wrong number or length of legs, too little, too much. According to the system of analogies that has been built up through the book, their bodies, like the body of the priest, are living, physical exemplars of the law.

Two conditions stand for the result of injustice, to be despoiled, that is to be the victim of theft or fraud, and to be oppressed, that is to carry a heavy burden (Isaiah: 'under the heavy loads'). The unfair loss on the one hand, and the unfair burden on the other, these are the condition of poverty. No need to go to Jerusalem to recognize the poor: beggars, anonymously crowding the steps of public buildings, watchful for scraps of alms, but ready to scuttle into the shadows at the first sign of aggression. As they hobble on bandaged feet, staggering along on crutches, clutching with maimed hands the bags they use for their pathetic scavenging, we can recognize the prophets' description of poor ground-down faces. Other poor are labourers, toiling under cruel loads.

Now, consider again the forbidden animals. Consider especially the insects, their hunched backs, consider the lumpy face of the chameleon and the high humped shell-encased tortoise or beetle. Remember the huge loads of the toiling ants. Recall the watchfulness of spiders and cockroaches, freezing into stillness or scuttering away at the first sign of intruders on their scavenging work, creeping into crevices and dark corners. Remember the blindness of worms and bats, the vulnerability of fish without scales. No wonder the Lord made them and found them good, they are great for reminding the people of Israel of his commands. It makes sense that they should not be eaten. They should be respected not because they are foul and filthy, but because they are emblematic victims. They are called abominations, but it is their condition that is abominable. Foul injustice reduces people to this pass. The Mishnaic idea that these creatures are forbidden because they are scavengers was right. Scavenging in itself is not wrong. Being a scavenger is no sin. What is wrong is an unjust society that commits its members to a life of scavenging. It seems we have been reading the message upside down.

Justice and mercy

What a wonderful book is Leviticus. It keeps us guessing till the end, but when we reach the end we see that the explanation was always there and has only to be spelled out. Now that we know that blemish has to do with unrighteousness, we can turn back to chapter 19, the great essay on equity. There we find 'something superfluous, or something lacking' (the language of the King James's version) which has been applied to the bodies of priests and the bodies of sacrificial animals. The wrongness of something superfluous or something missing is put in terms of just transactions. False measures are explicitly forbidden, and unfair weights. As well as stealing, robbing, defrauding, oppressing, lies and slander (19: 11–17), Leviticus forbids measures which give one party too much and the other too little (19: 33–36).

210

Now look at Isaiah's fulminations against injustice and now ask again whether it was fair to put priest and prophet on different sides of a line. The prophet sees the Lord manifest in justice, and so does the priest. The prophet uses poetry to speak for the Lord's righteousness and the priest shows righteousness depicted in creation. When the prophet says the Lord rejects sacrifice because blood is on the hands of the congregation, he never says there shall be no more sacrifices or sabbaths. He only says that sacrifice without justice angers the Lord. And he promises that Jerusalem will be known again as the city of righteousness. The Priests are saying that sacrifice and justice must be enacted together; they never say that the ritual enactment will be acceptable on its own, without the justice. Isaiah's words, 'Seek justice, correct oppression, defend the fatherless, plead for the widow' (1: 17), find their echo in Leviticus's chapters on mercy, justice and love. In the priestly vision the whole world and the whole book are based on justice. The idea that the cultic service will satisfy the Lord without regard for his justice is very far from their teaching.

I have explained how the anthropologist approaches religions and deals with variety. I have used anthropology to reread Leviticus with the result that the priestly editors are relieved of the charge of preferring ritual to justice. This result stems from the anthropologist's effort to detect bias and to correct it. The guiding principle is to expect that the religion as recorded in its sacred books is unitary. If the people of Israel thought that they were bound together by one religion, the anthropologist takes that belief seriously. We find that with their different emphases, prophets and priests are preaching the same faith.

Part of my argument has been to insist that each religion has its own 'physics', its ontological theory which gives the principles of time, space and all existence. This, I suspect, points to why believers may be ready to die for their religion. The outsider wonders, whence is their joy, and why all this rejoicing? The Bible gives the answer: like the dumb beasts, the people rejoice in living the sacred order. Like the worms and snakes, like the camel and the pig, the lizard and the spider, the law fulfils their own being. Refusing to see boiled lobster or crab on their festive table, the Jews honour the cosmic joke: the mighty are bowed down and the lowly are lifted up.

And I can conclude by asking for justice for the priestly editors:[1] sheer prejudice has depicted them as too solemn to join in the laughter.

Note

1 Numbers' opening words, 'In the wilderness', make a direct link between Mosaic law and the idea of the wilderness, the site of divine espousals renewed, the second betrothal of Israel, the mystic bride. See Mary Douglas (1993) *In the Wilderness: the Doctrine of Defilement in the Book of Numbers*. Sheffield: Academic Press.

Index